100 MOST FEARED CREATURES

Conceived, edited, and designed by Marshall Editions
The Old Brewery
6 Blundell Street
London N7 9BH

ISBN 978-0-545-56342-0

Publisher: Zeta Davies
Project Editor: Carey Scott
Designer: Dave Ball
Picture Researcher: Jean Hosking
Production: Nikki Ingram

Printed and bound in China by Toppan Leefung Printers Ltd.

10 9 8 7 6 5 4 3 2 1   13 14 15 16 17 18

First edition, September 2013

100 MOST FEARED CREATURES

Scholastic Inc.

CONTENTS

FEARSOME CREATURES

Watch out! The world is full of scary creatures that can sting, bite, poison, ram, or trample you if you annoy them or just get too close. They could be tiny, like the bullet ant, with its nightmarishly painful sting, or huge, like a charging elephant. Deadly animals live in all kinds of places, from the bottom of the sea to the attic of your house. Some even survive by burrowing inside you and munching on parts of your body!

Ahhhhhh! Help!

Don't worry too much! The good news is, most of these dangerous beasts will leave *you* alone if you leave *them* alone. They mainly live in faraway places, or safely tucked away in zoos. Luckily, there are medical treatments for most types of dangerous animal bites and stings.

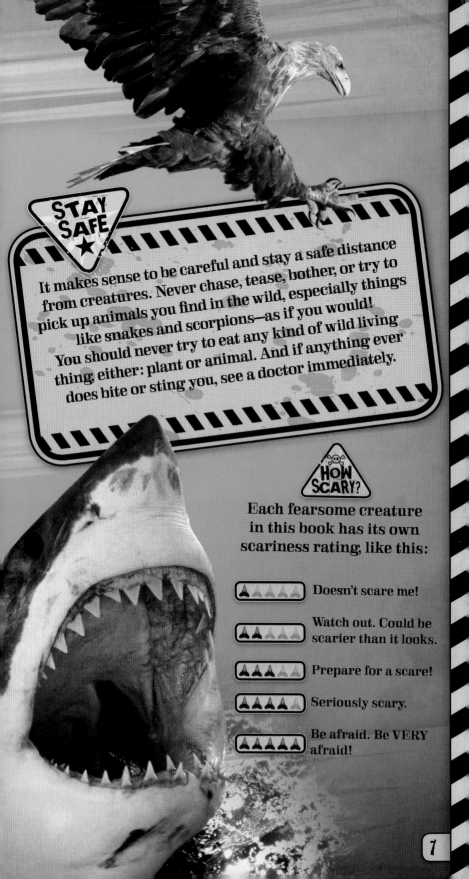

HOW SCARY?

Each fearsome creature in this book has its own scariness rating, like this:

▲▲▲▲▲ Doesn't scare me!

▲▲▲▲▲ Watch out. Could be scarier than it looks.

▲▲▲▲▲ Prepare for a scare!

▲▲▲▲▲ Seriously scary.

▲▲▲▲▲ Be afraid. Be VERY afraid!

VIPERS

There are more than 200 types, or species, of vipers, and they're all scarily venomous. With their long, sharp fangs and powerful bodies, most of them can bite fast and hard.

5

GABOON VIPER

LENGTH: 4–7 feet (1.2–2.2 m)

DEADLY WEAPONS: Fangs up to 2 inches (5 cm)—the longest of any venomous snake.

HOW SCARY?

SCARY SKILLS: Can swivel its eyes around to look in different directions.

4

RATTLESNAKE

LENGTH: 3–8 feet (1–2.4 m)

DEADLY WEAPONS: Powerful venom that eats away at flesh. Yuck!

SCARY SKILLS: Uses the rings of dried skin on its tail to make a spooky rattling sound as a warning.

HOW SCARY?

3

PUFF ADDER

LENGTH: 3–5 feet (1–1.5 m)

DEADLY WEAPONS: Extra-long fangs that can inject deep into the skin.

HOW SCARY?

SCARY SKILLS: Can inflate and puff up its body to look even scarier.

2

TERCIOPELO

LENGTH: 4–7 feet (1.2–2 m)

DEADLY WEAPONS: Like most vipers, the terciopelo has heat-sensing pits on its face that can detect prey by their body heat.

HOW SCARY?

SCARY SKILLS: Most snakes flee from danger, but the terciopelo is known to stand its ground and attack people!

RUSSELL'S VIPER

The brown, spotted Asian Russell's viper lives in farmers' fields, where people often disturb or step on it by mistake. When it bites, its venom causes terrible pain, swelling, and bleeding all over the body. Yikes! Medicine can save you, but many victims live too far from a hospital to get there in time.

LENGTH: 3–5.5 feet (1–1.6 m)

DEADLY WEAPONS: Powerful jaws that clamp tight and hang on after biting.

SCARY SKILLS: Can strike with so much speed and energy that it almost leaps into the air!

HOW SCARY?

KILLER FACT

Vipers can fold their venom-injecting fangs flat when they're not needed, then flick them forward in the blink of an eye—ready to strike.

COBRAS

Rearing up, swaying from side to side, and spreading out their necks into wide "hoods," cobras are well-known and widely feared in Asia and Africa, where they live.

5

FOREST COBRA

LENGTH: 4.9–9.8 feet (1.5–3 m)

DEADLY WEAPONS: Aggressive attitude and very toxic venom.

SCARY SKILLS: Unusually adaptable; can live in towns and climb trees.

HOW SCARY?

4

KING COBRA

HOW SCARY?

LENGTH: 8–18 feet (2.4–5.5 m)

DEADLY WEAPONS: Its huge size—this is the longest venomous snake in the entire world.

SCARY SKILLS: Its hiss makes a frightening growling noise!

3

HOW SCARY?

GIANT SPITTING COBRA

LENGTH: Around 9 feet (2.7 m)

DEADLY WEAPONS: Large venom glands that can inject a massive dose of deadly poison.

SCARY SKILLS: Can shoot a jet of blinding venom into enemies' eyes.

2

PHILIPPINE COBRA

LENGTH: 3–5.2 feet (1–1.6 m)

DEADLY WEAPONS: Deadliest venom of any cobra, causing paralysis and breathing problems within 30 minutes.

SCARY SKILLS: Can spit venom accurately a distance of up to 10 feet (3 m) away!

HOW SCARY?

SPECTACLED COBRA

Also called the Indian cobra, this snake is one of the most famous and feared in all of Asia. Thousands of people are bitten each year. Its venom acts so fast—stopping the heartbeat or the ability to breathe—that many don't survive.

LENGTH: 5–8 feet (1.5–2.4 m)

DEADLY WEAPONS: Killer venom and a bold attitude.

SCARY SKILLS: Spreads its "hood" to reveal spectacle-like markings on the back of its neck.

HOW SCARY?

▲▲▲▲▲

KILLER FACT
★

Cobras spread out their "hoods" by flattening out the rib bones in their necks. Unlike humans and most other animals, snakes have ribs all the way down their bodies.

SEA SNAKES

Did you know that some snakes live in the sea? They have flattened bodies and tails to help them swim, and deadly venom for attacking prey.

5

HOW SCARY?
▲▲▲▲△

BANDED SEA KRAIT

LENGTH: 2–5 feet (0.6–1.5 m)

DEADLY WEAPONS: Extremely deadly venom, though it rarely bites.

SCARY SKILLS: Watch out—this sea snake also comes ashore and climbs trees!

4

YELLOW-BELLIED SEA SNAKE

LENGTH: 2–3 feet (0.6–0.9 m)

DEADLY WEAPONS: Dangerously deadly venomous bite.

SCARY SKILLS: Can stay underwater for three hours before coming to the surface to breathe.

HOW SCARY?
▲▲▲▲△

3

OLIVE SEA SNAKE

LENGTH: 3–5 feet (0.9–1.6 m)

DEADLY WEAPONS: Its sharp fangs are the longest of all the sea snakes and can even bite through a wet suit.

SCARY SKILLS: Its tail can detect light, like an eye, but experts don't know what this is for!

HOW SCARY?
▲▲▲▲▲

2

STOKES' SEA SNAKE

LENGTH: 4–6 feet (1.2–1.8 m)

DEADLY WEAPONS: Big, bulky body gives it lots of strength.

SCARY SKILLS: Wraps itself around victims and holds on tight while biting them.

HOW SCARY?
▲▲▲▲▲

BEAKED SEA SNAKE

Most sea snakes are naturally shy, but the beaked sea snake is bad-tempered and aggressive. When it gets annoyed, it doesn't swim away, it attacks. That's unlucky, because the venom in just one bite from this sea snake is powerful enough to kill more than 50 people!

LENGTH: 2–5 feet (0.6–1.5 m)

DEADLY WEAPONS: Venom that experts believe is the most toxic of any sea snake.

SCARY SKILLS: Hides by lurking in shallow, muddy water near the shore.

HOW SCARY?

KILLER FACT

Sea snakes have thin, breakable fangs. If one bites you, its fangs can snap off and get stuck in your skin. Ouch!

ELAPID SNAKES

This family of snakes is found all over the world. Although elapid snakes have small, non-movable fangs, some of them are the deadliest and scariest snakes of all.

5

EASTERN CORAL SNAKE

HOW SCARY?

LENGTH: 1.5–3.5 feet (0.4–1.1 m)

DEADLY WEAPONS: Coral snakes have the deadliest venom of any snake in North America, where they live.

SCARY SKILLS: Burrows into the soil to hide.

4

DEATH ADDER

HOW SCARY?

LENGTH: 2–3 feet (0.6–0.9 m)

DEADLY WEAPONS: Extremely deadly venom.

SCARY SKILLS: Can use its narrow tail tip as bait to lure prey.

3

HOW SCARY?

INLAND TAIPAN

LENGTH: 5–8 feet (1.5–2.4 m)

DEADLY WEAPONS: Most toxic venom of any land snake on Earth—one bite has enough to kill 100 people.

SCARY SKILLS: Changes color through the year, making it hard to recognize.

2

COMMON KRAIT

LENGTH: 2–6 feet (0.6–1.8 m)

DEADLY WEAPONS: Venom more toxic than a cobra's, making it one of India's most feared snakes.

SCARY SKILLS: Becomes active at night, when it may sneak into houses and even beds!

HOW SCARY?

BLACK MAMBA

Be afraid—be very afraid! This massive, fast, deadly African snake is one of the most dangerous and feared snakes on the planet. It can move at lightning speed and bite many times over. Without treatment, a black mamba bite can kill in just 20 minutes.

LENGTH: 7–15 feet (2–4.5 m)

DEADLY WEAPONS: It has not only superpowerful venom, but is also incredibly fierce.

SCARY SKILLS: Fastest snake on land, slithering along at speeds of up to 12.5 mph (20 km/h).

HOW SCARY?
▲▲▲▲▲

KILLER FACT ★

The black mamba gets its name from its deep black throat and tongue, which it shows when angry.

COLUBRID SNAKES

The colubrids are the biggest snake family, with almost 2,000 species. They don't inject much venom, and few colubrids are dangerous, but there are exceptions. . . .

5 BROWN TREE SNAKE

LENGTH: 3–6 feet (0.9–1.8 m)

DEADLY WEAPONS: Venomous enough to harm a child.

SCARY SKILLS: Rears up angrily if cornered.

HOW SCARY?

4 TIGER KEELBACK

LENGTH: 2–3 feet (0.6–0.8 m)

DEADLY WEAPONS: Very toxic venom.

SCARY SKILLS: It uses poisonous chemicals from the toads it eats to fend off predators.

HOW SCARY?

3 BIRD SNAKE

LENGTH: 2.5–4.5 feet (0.8–1.4 m)

DEADLY WEAPONS: Deadly bite with no known treatment, although it rarely bites.

SCARY SKILLS: Excellent at camouflage—looks exactly like a twig when in a tree.

HOW SCARY?

2 FOREST VINE SNAKE

LENGTH: 3–5.5 feet (1–1.6 m)

DEADLY WEAPONS: One of the most venomous African snakes.

SCARY SKILLS: When it bites, it holds on and chews to release as much venom as possible.

HOW SCARY?

BOOMSLANG

The boomslang is the world's most feared colubrid snake. It is a large, tree-climbing snake of differing colors, with huge black eyes. Like other colubrids, it is not aggressive but its bite can kill. A boomslang's venom is slow to act, so victims may think they are unharmed—until it's too late!

LENGTH: 4–7 feet (1.2–2 m)

DEADLY WEAPONS: Dangerous venom that may not have symptoms at first, but then causes bleeding from all the body's openings.

SCARY SKILLS: Can inflate its neck like a balloon to make itself look bigger.

HOW SCARY?

KILLER FACT

Victims of boomslang bites may need blood transfusions. If left untreated, they can bleed to death.

CONSTRICTORS

These snakes kill by constricting, or squeeeeeezing, their prey tightly to stop it from breathing. Once the victim is dead, the snake swallows it whole.

5

BOA CONSTRICTOR

LENGTH: 3–13 feet (1–4 m)

DEADLY WEAPONS: Though it doesn't kill by biting, an angry boa can give you a nasty nip.

SCARY SKILLS: The boa constrictor is extremely strong—strong enough to squeeze the life out of its prey.

4

BURMESE PYTHON

LENGTH: 10–23 feet (3–7 m)

DEADLY WEAPONS: Like other snakes, has jaws that can open much wider than its head to devour large prey animals whole.

SCARY SKILLS: Good at swimming and often hides underwater.

3

AFRICAN ROCK PYTHON

LENGTH: 13–20 feet (4–6 m)

DEADLY WEAPONS: Very big and strong; it is Africa's largest snake.

SCARY SKILLS: Heat sensors on its jaws and a smell-sensing tongue to detect prey.

2

RETICULATED PYTHON

LENGTH: 10–30 feet (3–9 m)

DEADLY WEAPONS: The world's longest snake.

SCARY SKILLS: Able to swallow animals as large as wild pigs, deer, and sometimes humans—gulp!

GREEN ANACONDA

The green anaconda of South America is the world's biggest, heaviest, and strongest snake. If it decided to coil around and constrict you, there'd be no escape! Green anacondas are water lovers and enjoy lurking and slithering around in swamps and shallow rivers.

LENGTH: 20–30 feet (6–9 m)

DEADLY WEAPONS: Big, powerful head and jaws so it can grab prey before wrapping around it.

SCARY SKILLS: Can survive for months between meals.

HOW SCARY?

KILLER FACT

After a meal, a constrictor lies still while strong chemicals in its stomach completely dissolve and digest the prey—even the bones, teeth, skin, and horns!

CROCODILES AND ALLIGATORS

This group of snapping water reptiles includes crocodiles, caimans, gharials, and alligators. Plenty of people have ended up inside the larger and fiercer types.

5 AMERICAN CROCODILE

LENGTH: 8–15 feet (2.4–4.6 m)

DEADLY WEAPONS: Sharp, conical teeth and large claws.

SCARY SKILLS: Can hide underwater with only its eyes and nostrils visible.

HOW SCARY?

4 BLACK CAIMAN

LENGTH: 10–20 feet (3–6 m)

DEADLY WEAPONS: Great size and strength allow it to attack large prey.

SCARY SKILLS: Very good eyesight and hearing for hunting at night.

HOW SCARY?

3 AMERICAN ALLIGATOR

LENGTH: 5.5–13 feet (1.7–4 m)

DEADLY WEAPONS: Big, wide jaws with enormous biting strength.

SCARY SKILLS: Uses its powerful tail to lunge out of the water to catch prey on the bank.

HOW SCARY?

2 NILE CROCODILE

LENGTH: 10–20 feet (3–6 m)

DEADLY WEAPONS: Huge, powerful tail that can be used to round up fish to eat.

SCARY SKILLS: Like other crocs, it thrashes violently to tear prey to pieces.

HOW SCARY?

SALTWATER CROCODILE

The saltwater crocodile, or "saltie," is the biggest crocodile, and the biggest reptile, in the world. The saltie is thought to gobble up several people a year, mainly in Australia. It can leap forward and grab its prey so fast that there's no time to escape.

LENGTH: 9–23 feet (2.7–7 m)

DEADLY WEAPONS: Very long and large jaws, making it extremely dangerous to humans.

SCARY SKILLS: Can live in salt water as well as rivers and swamps, so it often swims out to sea.

HOW SCARY?

▲▲▲▲▲

KILLER FACT
★

Crocodiles and alligators usually slither along on their bellies, but can also run at speeds of up to 12 miles per hour (19 km/h).

LIZARDS

Many lizards are small, and some are even cute. But there are also some strange, scary, and positively monstrous ones out there!

5 TEXAS HORNED LIZARD

LENGTH: 2.5–4 inches (6.4–10 cm)

DEADLY WEAPONS: It looks like a spiky dinosaur, but this lizard is pretty small, and only really deadly to the insects it hunts.

SCARY SKILLS: Squirts blood at its enemies from its eyes!

HOW SCARY?

4 GILA MONSTER

LENGTH: 0.5–2 feet (0.4–0.6 m)

DEADLY WEAPONS: A very painful, venomous bite.

SCARY SKILLS: After biting, it latches on and chews hard—ouch!

HOW SCARY?

3 NILE MONITOR LIZARD

LENGTH: 6–8 feet (0.8–2.4 m)

DEADLY WEAPONS: Sharp teeth and claws and a huge, lashing tail.

SCARY SKILLS: Can sniff out prey with its forked tongue, just like a snake.

HOW SCARY?

2 MEXICAN BEADED LIZARD

LENGTH: 2–3 feet (0.6–0.9 m)

DEADLY WEAPONS: Dangerous bite that can kill a human by causing breathing problems.

SCARY SKILLS: The beaded lizard is immune to its own venom.

HOW SCARY?

KOMODO DRAGON

The biggest lizard on Earth is a drooling, dinosaur-like beast that can swim, dig up bones, kill prey larger than itself, and may attack humans. Though it's not actually a dragon, the Komodo dragon does look like a mythical monster. It is a very scary beast.

LENGTH: 5–10 feet (1.5–3 m)

DEADLY WEAPONS: Huge jaws and claws and a fatal, bacteria-filled bite.

SCARY SKILLS: Can gobble up almost its entire body weight in one go.

HOW SCARY?

KILLER FACT

Komodo dragons can be cannibalistic, meaning they will eat other Komodos. They are likely to prey on young, old, or sick ones.

FROGS

Most frogs are harmless, but there are a few you should watch out for. These are the tiny, colorful, but deadly poisonous frogs whose skin contains powerful toxins.

5 SPLASH-BACKED POISON FROG

LENGTH: 0.75 inch (2 cm)

DEADLY WEAPONS: The poison in its skin could kill up to five people.

SCARY SKILLS: Like other frogs, it shoots out its long, sticky tongue to catch insects.

HOW SCARY?

4 PHANTASMAL POISON FROG

LENGTH: 0.5 inch (1 cm)

DEADLY WEAPONS: Scientists have found that its poison can also be used to make a powerful painkiller.

SCARY SKILLS: Males can stand up and fight each other with their front legs.

HOW SCARY?

3 KOKOE POISON DART FROG

LENGTH: 1–1.25 inch (2.5–3 cm)

DEADLY WEAPONS: If touched, its toxic skin causes horrible pain, fever, and then paralysis.

SCARY SKILLS: Makes a high-pitched call that sounds like a bird.

HOW SCARY?

2 BLACK-LEGGED DART FROG

LENGTH: Around 2 inches (5 cm)

DEADLY WEAPONS: This frog's poison has killed humans by paralyzing them so they can't breathe.

SCARY SKILLS: Males carry their tadpoles by gluing them onto their backs!

HOW SCARY?

GOLDEN POISON DART FROG

This bright yellow or golden frog is the most dangerous frog of all. Its poison is among the deadliest of any animal—the toxic slime in one golden poison dart frog's skin could kill up to ten humans. You should never touch one—or even anything that one has touched!

LENGTH: Around 2 inches (5 cm)

DEADLY WEAPONS: Besides its deadly skin, it has a toothlike bone on its jaw.

SCARY SKILLS: Has sticky pads on its feet to help it climb.

HOW SCARY?

KILLER FACT

In South America, some indigenous people rub their darts on poison frogs' backs to pick up the poison.

TOADS AND SALAMANDERS

Toads, salamanders, and newts, which are part of the salamander family, have deadly poisons in their skin and are brightly colored to warn predators of the danger.

5

ROUGH-SKINNED NEWT

LENGTH: 5–8 inches (12–20 cm)

DEADLY WEAPONS: Poisonous skin slime that can burn if touched, and kill if swallowed.

SCARY SKILLS: Sneaks up on prey, then suddenly snaps it up.

HOW SCARY?

4

SPANISH RIBBED NEWT

LENGTH: 8–12 inches (20–30 cm)

DEADLY WEAPONS: Orange warts along the newt's sides release poison, but it isn't very harmful to humans.

SCARY SKILLS: Sharp ribs puncture its sides to create poison-tipped spines!

HOW SCARY?

3

FIRE SALAMANDER

LENGTH: 8–12 inches (20–30 cm)

DEADLY WEAPONS: Releases paralyzing poison around its neck and back when attacked.

SCARY SKILLS: Has a sticky tongue to help it catch prey.

HOW SCARY?

2

FIRE-BELLIED TOAD

LENGTH: 1–2 inches (3–5 cm)

DEADLY WEAPONS: Poison-releasing glands behind the head.

SCARY SKILLS: When threatened, the toad flips its front and back ends up to show its bright orange belly.

HOW SCARY?

CANE TOAD

The huge, heavy, and warty cane toad is not usually deadly to humans, but, wherever it goes, animals such as snakes and lizards die from trying to eat it. Dogs and other pets are often poisoned to death by cane toads.

LENGTH: 4–6 inches (10–15 cm)

DEADLY WEAPONS: Releases milky-looking, deadly poisonous liquid from glands on its neck.

SCARY SKILLS: Will fight attackers by trying to rub its poison glands on them!

HOW SCARY?

KILLER FACT

The poison glands under their skin make toads look warty, but touching them won't give you warts!

REQUIEM SHARKS

Requiem sharks are a family of mostly large, fierce, and fast species, several of which are dangerous. They have long, streamlined bodies, pointed snouts, and large tails.

5 LEMON SHARK

HOW SCARY? ▲▲▲

LENGTH: 8–10 feet (2.4–3 m)

DEADLY WEAPONS: Very powerful bite. Occasionally attacks humans.

SCARY SKILLS: Uses its yellowish-gray skin to camouflage itself on sandy seabeds.

4 BLUE SHARK

LENGTH: 6–12 feet (1.8–3.7 m)

DEADLY WEAPONS: Superfast swimming speed of up to 43 mph (69 km/h).

SCARY SKILLS: Extra-large eyes give it excellent eyesight.

HOW SCARY? ▲▲▲▲▲

3 OCEANIC WHITETIP SHARK

HOW SCARY? ▲▲▲▲

LENGTH: 5–14 feet (1.5–4 m)

DEADLY WEAPONS: Big, strong jaws and teeth.

SCARY SKILLS: Stubborn—will keep returning to attack prey again and again.

2 BULL SHARK

LENGTH: 7–11 feet (2–3.3 m)

DEADLY WEAPONS: Slicing teeth that tear prey as the shark thrashes about.

SCARY SKILLS: Can swim out of the sea and up into rivers and lakes, where it may attack swimmers.

HOW SCARY? ▲▲▲▲▲

TIGER SHARK

Of all the requiem sharks, the huge, hungry tiger shark is probably the scariest. Once it gets a whiff of something tasty—usually squid, turtles, or seals, but sometimes humans—it will stop at nothing to track it down and gobble it up.

LENGTH: 9–14 feet (2.7–4 m)

DEADLY WEAPONS: Very large, sharp teeth.

SCARY SKILLS: Will attack and eat almost anything, making it a very dangerous shark.

HOW SCARY?

▲▲▲▲▲

KILLER FACT
★

Some requiem sharks gather around disasters at sea, such as plane crashes and shipwrecks, to look for tasty snacks.

MACKEREL AND HAMMERHEAD SHARKS

This shark group includes some of the monsters of the shark world, including the much-feared great white, which is responsible for many of the shark attacks on humans.

SAND TIGER SHARK

5

HOW SCARY?

LENGTH: 8–11 feet (2.4–3.4 m)

DEADLY WEAPONS: A mouth full of scary, snaggle teeth, though it actually rarely bites humans.

SCARY SKILLS: Likes to gobble up its prey whole.

SMOOTH HAMMERHEAD

4

HOW SCARY?

LENGTH: 7–13 feet (2–4 m)

DEADLY WEAPONS: Like other hammerheads', its strange, wide head helps it scan the seabed for prey.

SCARY SKILLS: Hunts in large groups, called "schools" or "shivers."

GREAT HAMMERHEAD

3

HOW SCARY?

LENGTH: 7–20 feet (2–6 m)

DEADLY WEAPONS: The largest hammerhead.

SCARY SKILLS: Uses its wide head to pin down its favorite food, stingrays, while munching them to bits.

SHORTFIN MAKO SHARK

2

LENGTH: 10–13 feet (3–4 m)

DEADLY WEAPONS: Extremely sharp teeth, which it sometimes uses to bite divers.

SCARY SKILLS: This athletic shark can leap up to 20 feet (6 m) into the air.

HOW SCARY?

GREAT WHITE SHARK

The great white is the biggest predatory shark in all the oceans. It is one of a few shark species that can stick its head out of the water before and during attacks on prey. Its mouth is so massive that it can eat a whole sea lion in one bite!

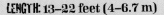

LENGTH: 13–22 feet (4–6.7 m)

DEADLY WEAPONS: Huge jaw, very large teeth, and strong, forceful bites.

SCARY SKILLS: Like other sharks, it can find prey by detecting electrical signals in victims' bodies.

HOW SCARY?

KILLER FACT

Experts think that great white attacks on humans occur because the shark mistakes a human swimmer for its usual seal prey.

FIERCE FISH

Sharks aren't the only fish that sometimes want an arm or a leg for lunch. Whether you're swimming in the sea or paddling in a river, watch out for these water monsters!

5

MORAY EEL

LENGTH: Up to 10 feet (3 m)

DEADLY WEAPONS: Huge jaws and teeth, with a second pair of jaws in its throat—yuck!

SCARY SKILLS: Lurks in crevices and caves, waiting for prey to pass by.

4

TIGER FISH

LENGTH: 3–5 feet (1–1.5 m)

DEADLY WEAPONS: Scarily long and sharp cone-shaped teeth.

SCARY SKILLS: Brave enough to fight crocodiles!

3

PIRANHA

LENGTH: 6–18 inches (15–46 cm)

DEADLY WEAPONS: Supersharp teeth for slicing meat off bones.

SCARY SKILLS: Gathers in groups, or shoals, to devour large animals in a feeding frenzy.

2

BARRACUDA

LENGTH: Up to 7 feet (2 m)

DEADLY WEAPONS: Superspeedy barracudas swim fast and attack quickly.

SCARY SKILLS: Will attack anything silvery or sparkly, so don't wear jewelry when diving!

GOONCH

The mighty goonch, a giant catfish living in the great rivers of Asia, is known as the "man-eating catfish" for good reason. Some people think these fish may have learned to like the taste of human flesh after feeding on dead bodies on funeral pyres that sometimes float on rivers in India.

LENGTH: 5–7 feet (1.5–2 m)

DEADLY WEAPONS: Backward-pointing teeth that grip prey so it can't escape.

SCARY SKILLS: Is thought to be able to sniff out human flesh. Yikes!

HOW SCARY?

KILLER FACT

The goonch may have dragged human swimmers underwater to drown them.

SPINY FISH

Some of the world's most dangerous fish don't attack by biting. Instead, they have seriously scary spines that they can jab into their victims to inject killer venom.

5

HOW SCARY?

SURGEONFISH

LENGTH: 6–20 inches (15–51 cm)

DEADLY WEAPONS: Razor-sharp, bladelike, and often venomous spines around the tail.

SCARY SKILLS: Thrashes its tail from side to side to slice and slash at enemies.

4

PUFFER FISH

LENGTH: 1–35 inches (2.5–90 cm)

DEADLY WEAPONS: Poisonous, spiny skin; sharp, biting teeth; and deadly poisonous if eaten.

SCARY SKILLS: Inflates itself with air or water to turn into a round, spiky ball.

HOW SCARY?

3

STINGRAY

LENGTH: 0.8–14 feet (0.3–5.4 m)

DEADLY WEAPONS: Sharp, venomous spine, or sting, in the tail.

SCARY SKILLS: Flicks its sting upward suddenly to jab enemies.

HOW SCARY?

2

LIONFISH

LENGTH: 12–15 inches (30–38 cm)

DEADLY WEAPONS: Long fin spines that deliver horribly painful, occasionally deadly venom.

SCARY SKILLS: Rounds up prey by wrapping long, spiny fins around victims.

HOW SCARY?

STONEFISH

It is an easy mistake to stand on a stonefish, because it looks just like a stone in shallow water. But its sting is so painful that victims have been known to beg to have their foot chopped off! The venom injected by this fish's stinging spines can be deadly if untreated.

LENGTH: 12–18 inches (30–46 cm)

DEADLY WEAPONS: 13 back spines that inject agonizingly painful, killer venom.

SCARY SKILLS: Brilliant camouflage that makes it look like a bumpy, speckled stone on the seabed.

HOW SCARY?

KILLER FACT

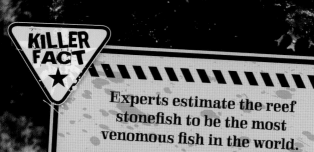

Experts estimate the reef stonefish to be the most venomous fish in the world.

SPIKE-NOSED FISH

These fearsome fish have long, sharp spikes, swords, or saws on their snouts. These can be used as deadly weapons when they are attacked.

5 SAILFISH

LENGTH: 5–11 feet (1.5–3.4 m)

DEADLY WEAPONS: Very sharp, pointed spike or bill for stabbing at prey.

SCARY SKILLS: Can change color, from brown or gray to purple or silver, in an instant.

HOW SCARY?

4 SAWFISH

HOW SCARY?

LENGTH: 15–22 feet (4.5–6.7 m)

DEADLY WEAPONS: Long, wide, sawlike snout edged with dozens of sharp teeth.

SCARY SKILLS: Slashing its saw sideways to swipe at prey.

3 NEEDLEFISH

LENGTH: Up to 4 feet (1.2 m)

DEADLY WEAPONS: Extremely sharp, needlelike snout.

SCARY SKILLS: Leaping out of the water over boats, sometimes spearing and killing those on board.

HOW SCARY?

2 SWORDFISH

HOW SCARY?

LENGTH: 4–15 feet (1.2–4.5 m)

DEADLY WEAPONS: Sharp, sturdy "sword" on snout, strong enough to ram through the side of a boat.

SCARY SKILLS: Leaping high out of the water.

BLUE MARLIN

The marlin is one of the hardest and most dangerous fish to catch. Incredibly strong and fast, if a marlin is dragged ashore or onto a boat, it will fight back by thrashing and slashing with its sword. In 2000, a fisherman was killed this way.

LENGTH: 10–16 feet (3–5 m)

DEADLY WEAPONS: Narrow, very sharp bill that can be over 3 feet (1 m) long.

SCARY SKILLS: Great strength and fighting power.

HOW SCARY?

KILLER FACT

Marlin and sailfish are the world's fastest fish, capable of speeding through the water at around 65 miles per hour (100 km/h).

JELLYFISH

Some of these strange sea creatures swim, but others just float around with the sea currents, waiting for prey to become entangled in their stinging tentacles.

5

SEA NETTLE

LENGTH: 6–8 inches (15–20 cm) across; tentacles up to 20 inches (50 cm) long

DEADLY WEAPONS: Thousands of tiny stinging cells, inject painful venom if touched.

SCARY SKILLS: Swims by squeezing its bell-shaped body in and out.

HOW SCARY?

4

PORTUGUESE MAN-OF-WAR

LENGTH: 8–12 inches (20–30 cm) across; tentacles up to 160 feet (50 m) long

DEADLY WEAPONS: Tentacles' sting can cause extreme pain.

SCARY SKILLS: Gas-filled blue bladder enables it to float on the surface.

HOW SCARY?

3

IRUKANDJI

LENGTH: 0.5–1.5 inches (2–3 cm) across; tentacles up to 20 inches (50 cm) long

DEADLY WEAPONS: Deadly venom that causes sickness, backache, and vomiting. It can be fatal.

SCARY SKILLS: The sting causes little pain at first, so victims don't know they've been stung.

HOW SCARY?

2

HABU JELLY

LENGTH: About 7 inches (18 cm) across; tentacles up to 9 feet (3 m)

DEADLY WEAPONS: Venom that causes shock, paralysis, and even death.

SCARY SKILLS: Fast swimmer; tentacles tangle around prey.

HOW SCARY?

AUSTRALIAN BOX JELLY

The Australian box jelly, sometimes called the sea wasp, is the world's most venomous and feared jellyfish. When its tentacles touch something, they release their deadly venom instantly. Victims can suffer a heart attack within minutes of being stung.

LENGTH: 6–14 inches (15–36 cm) across; tentacles up to 10 feet (3 m) long

DEADLY WEAPONS: Up to 60 long tentacles, covered with millions of stinging cells.

SCARY SKILLS: Almost completely see-through, making it hard to see this jellyfish coming!

HOW SCARY?

KILLER FACT

No jellyfish has brains, but the box jellyfish is the only one to have eyes—24 of them!

OCTOPUSES AND SQUID

These animals' class name is Cephalopoda, meaning "head feet," as their tentacles are joined to their heads. They can grow to be huge, and are very clever.

GIANT PACIFIC OCTOPUS

5

HOW SCARY? ☠ ▲▲▲△△

LENGTH: 10–16 feet (3–5 m)

DEADLY WEAPONS: A venomous bite, though it's not harmful to humans.

SCARY SKILLS: Big and strong enough to pull off the masks and breathing gear of divers, though this is rare.

GIANT SQUID

4

HOW SCARY? ☠ ▲▲▲△△

LENGTH: Up to 50 feet (15 m)

DEADLY WEAPONS: Tentacles covered in powerful, razor-edged suckers.

SCARY SKILLS: Amazing eyesight, thanks to its enormous eyes.

COLOSSAL SQUID

3

HOW SCARY? ☠ ▲▲▲△△

LENGTH: Up to 43 feet (14 m)

DEADLY WEAPONS: Sharp, rotating hooks on its tentacles for hooking into prey.

SCARY SKILLS: So big and strong, it can easily grab a human.

HUMBOLDT SQUID

2

HOW SCARY? ☠ ▲▲▲▲△

LENGTH: 4–7 feet (1.2–2 m)

DEADLY WEAPONS: Powerful biting beak for tearing at flesh.

SCARY SKILLS: Hunts in shoals to catch large prey; may attack humans.

BLUE-RINGED OCTOPUS

The most dangerous of all cephalopods is one of the tiniest—the blue-ringed octopus. This creature is so small, it could sit in your hand, but it has a seriously venomous bite that can kill a human in minutes. Victims often don't feel the bite, so there may be little time to get help.

HOW SCARY?

▲▲▲▲▲

LENGTH: 4–6 inches (10–15 cm)

DEADLY WEAPONS: Killer venom that paralyzes victims and stops them from breathing.

SCARY SKILLS: Turns bright yellow with flashing blue rings when it's about to attack.

KILLER FACT
★

Almost all cephalopods can shoot an inky liquid onto predators to confuse them. In Italy, the ink is eaten as a pasta sauce!

ECHINODERMS

This group of spiny-skinned sea creatures includes sea urchins and starfish. They are usually round or star-shaped, and move around slowly on the seabed.

5 COMMON SUNSTAR

LENGTH: 8–14 inches (20–35 cm) across

DEADLY WEAPONS: Covered in stinging bristles, which are not deadly but can give a human a nasty rash.

HOW SCARY?

SCARY SKILLS: Like other starfish, turns its stomach inside out to devour its prey.

4 BLACK LONG-SPINED SEA URCHIN

LENGTH: 4–24 inches (10–60 cm) across (including the spines)

DEADLY WEAPONS: Very sharp, long spines that can easily pierce skin and break off inside.

SCARY SKILLS: Waves and shakes its spines around when disturbed.

HOW SCARY?

3 CROWN-OF-THORNS STARFISH

LENGTH: 8–18 inches (20–46 cm) across

DEADLY WEAPONS: Sharp spines that deliver horribly painful venom.

HOW SCARY?

SCARY SKILLS: Destroys coral reefs by gobbling them up.

2 SEA CUCUMBER

LENGTH: 0.75–18 inches (2–20 cm)

DEADLY WEAPONS: Squirts out sticky, toxic threads that can cause blindness if they touch your eyes.

HOW SCARY?

SCARY SKILLS: Can turn its body to liquid and pour itself through tiny cracks!

FLOWER URCHIN

If you're ever snorkeling and you spot this attractive, flowerlike sea urchin, DO NOT TOUCH IT! Its "petals" can inject very nasty venom into anything they brush against. The pain is so bad, it can make divers panic, putting them in great danger.

LENGTH: 4–6 inches (10–15 cm) across

DEADLY WEAPONS: Covered in cup-shaped pincers that can give you a dangerous sting.

SCARY SKILLS: The "petals" work like tiny jaws that snap shut to inject their venom.

HOW SCARY?

KILLER FACT

Although they are not deadly, a flower urchin sting can knock a person unconscious or paralyze him or her with pain.

ELECTRIC FISH

Humans have been using electricity for only a couple of hundred years, but these shocking fish have been zapping their enemies since prehistoric times!

5 — OCELLATED ELECTRIC RAY

LENGTH: Up to 10 inches (25 cm)

DEADLY WEAPONS: Gives off weak electricity that can put off some predators.

SCARY SKILLS: Perfectly camouflaged on the sandy seabed.

HOW SCARY?

4 — STARGAZER

LENGTH: 8–18 inches (20–46 cm)

DEADLY WEAPONS: Can give a human a painful, though not serious, electric shock.

SCARY SKILLS: Also jabs enemies with its venomous spines.

HOW SCARY?

3 — ATLANTIC TORPEDO

LENGTH: 5–6 feet (1.5–1.8 m)

DEADLY WEAPONS: Delivers up to 220 volts of electricity, enough to knock a human over.

SCARY SKILLS: Can zap enemies with a series of repeated electrical "pulses."

HOW SCARY?

2 — ELECTRIC CATFISH

LENGTH: 2–4 feet (0.6–1.2 m)

DEADLY WEAPONS: Electric organ all around its body that can zap a person with up to 450 volts.

SCARY SKILLS: Can also use its electricity as a kind of radar to hunt down prey.

HOW SCARY?

ELECTRIC EEL

The electric eel, found in rivers in South America, is the most powerful of all electric fish. It can give a person enough shocks to be deadly. If victims are not killed by the shocks, they may fall unconscious and drown in the water.

LENGTH: 5–8 feet (1.6–2.4 m)

DEADLY WEAPONS: Can electrocute enemies with a 600-volt electric shock.

SCARY SKILLS: Electricity-proof skin saves the eels from shocking themselves!

HOW SCARY?
▲▲▲▲▲

KILLER FACT
★ The ancient Egyptians and Greeks used electric fish to shock patients as a way of trying to treat aches, pains, and diseases.

SURPRISINGLY SCARY SEA CREATURES

Some sea animals are really scary looking, and others look harmless but are actually deadly dangerous. Beware of these snails, slugs, and sea anemones!

5 AMERICAN LOBSTER

LENGTH: 12–40 inches (30–100 cm)

DEADLY WEAPONS: Huge pincers lined with teeth for crushing and cutting prey.

SCARY SKILLS: Pincer power strong enough to crush a human's fingers.

HOW SCARY?

4 FIRE CORAL

LENGTH: 2–24 inches (5–61 cm)

DEADLY WEAPONS: Stinging cells, similar to those on a jellyfish.

SCARY SKILLS: Can cause a nasty, painful rash that can last for weeks.

HOW SCARY?

3 HELL'S FIRE ANEMONE

LENGTH: 8–12 inches (20–30 cm) across

DEADLY WEAPONS: Powerful stinging cells that can cause shock and pain in victims.

SCARY SKILLS: Camouflaged by a bumpy surface that looks like coral seaweed.

HOW SCARY?

2 BLUE SEA SLUG

LENGTH: 1–1.5 inches (2–3 cm)

DEADLY WEAPONS: Over 30 fingerlike tentacles, each with a terrifyingly lethal sting.

SCARY SKILLS: Eats the much larger Portuguese man-of-war jellyfish and collects its venom.

HOW SCARY?

GEOGRAPHER CONE

You may have admired beautiful seashells like this. But the creature that lives in this shell is one of the scariest in the sea. The geographer cone is a sea snail with a deadly harpoonlike weapon, which it darts out to jab its enemies with a deadly sting.

LENGTH: 4–6 inches (10–15 cm)

DEADLY WEAPONS: A spearlike tooth that it uses to inject its deadly venom into its victim.

SCARY SKILLS: Can reach its stomach out and wrap it around its prey.

HOW SCARY?

KILLER FACT ★

Geographer cone venom is so powerful that just one snail is capable of killing 700 people.

WHALES AND DOLPHINS

This family includes the biggest creatures on our planet. Yet they are usually friendly to humans. But whales and dolphins have been known to attack.

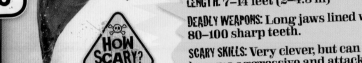

5

BOTTLENOSE DOLPHIN

LENGTH: 7–14 feet (2–4.3 m)

DEADLY WEAPONS: Long jaws lined with 80–100 sharp teeth.

SCARY SKILLS: Very clever, but can become aggressive and attack one another, or humans.

HOW SCARY?

4

SOUTHERN RIGHT WHALE

LENGTH: 33–60 feet (10–18 m)

DEADLY WEAPONS: Enormous size and strength.

SCARY SKILLS: Has been known to leap up out of the sea and crash onto boats—probably by accident.

HOW SCARY?

3

SHORT-FINNED PILOT WHALE

HOW SCARY?

LENGTH: 14–20 feet (4–6 m)

DEADLY WEAPONS: Very large mouth with strong, sturdy teeth.

SCARY SKILLS: Has been known to drag divers underwater—experts think to try to play with them.

2

KILLER WHALE

LENGTH: 16–33 feet (5–10 m)

DEADLY WEAPONS: Big, sharp, interlocking teeth for grabbing and slicing prey.

SCARY SKILLS: Hunts in shoals and has been known to kill humans when kept in captivity.

HOW SCARY?

SPERM WHALE

The sperm whale is a monster of the sea—the biggest of all the toothed whales on Earth. Sperm whales tackle large prey, such as giant squid, and have vicious fights with them deep underwater. In the past, people used to hunt sperm whales. They were dangerous targets, as they used their massive bodies to defend themselves.

LENGTH: 26–66 feet (8–20 m)

DEADLY WEAPONS: Humongous teeth that can grow to 8 inches (20 cm) long and weigh 2 pounds (1 kg) each.

SCARY SKILLS: May be able to zap and stun its prey with powerful beams of sound.

HOW SCARY?

▲▲▲▲▲

KILLER FACT

In 1820, an angry sperm whale rammed and sank an American whaling ship. The incident became the inspiration for the famous novel *Moby-Dick*.

SEALS AND SEA LIONS

They often look cute and cuddly with their chubby bodies and fluffy fur, but seals and sea lions can also be fast-moving and fierce, especially underwater.

5

GRAY SEAL

LENGTH: 7–10 feet (2–3 m)

DEADLY WEAPONS: Very sharp teeth with a surprisingly serious bite.

SCARY SKILLS: Has been known to drag swimmers underwater.

HOW SCARY?

4

SEA LION

LENGTH: 4–8 feet (1.2–2.4 m)

DEADLY WEAPONS: Very big, strong flippers.

SCARY SKILLS: Can leap up out of the sea, on one occasion to grab an unfortunate surfer!

HOW SCARY?

3

WALRUS

LENGTH: 7–12 feet (2–3.7 m)

DEADLY WEAPONS: Enormous, sharp tusks that can grow to up to 3 feet (1 m) long.

HOW SCARY?

SCARY SKILLS: Attacks and stabs with its tusks. Has occasionally killed hunters and attacked boats.

2

SOUTHERN ELEPHANT SEAL

LENGTH: 9–20 feet (2.7–6 m)

DEADLY WEAPONS: Huge mouth, great weight and strength.

SCARY SKILLS: Can lunge at its enemies, crushing them flat.

HOW SCARY?

LEOPARD SEAL

Though not the biggest, this is probably the fiercest of all seals, and is known to be dangerous to humans. It zooms through the sea as it hunts for penguins and squid. It can slither across sea ice, too. Its enormous head and jaws mean it can easily inflict a deadly bite.

LENGTH: 9–13 feet (2.5–4 m)

DEADLY WEAPONS: Massive, wide mouth full of large teeth with powerful biting strength.

SCARY SKILLS: Has been reported to chase explorers across sea ice!

HOW SCARY?
▲▲▲▲▲

KILLER FACT
★

A huge male elephant seal in New Zealand, nicknamed Homer, made a habit of coming ashore and ramming and crushing cars!

BEARS

Bears prefer foods like eggs, honey, berries, and fish. But they are such big, strong, fierce animals that if a bear gets annoyed, it can be very dangerous to humans.

AMERICAN BLACK BEAR

5

LENGTH: 4–7 feet (1.2–2 m)

DEADLY WEAPONS: Very strong, with a powerful bite.

SCARY SKILLS: Good at using its paws to open box lids, gates, and doors.

HOW SCARY?

ASIAN BLACK BEAR

4

LENGTH: 4–7 feet (1.2–2 m)

DEADLY WEAPONS: Large, hooked claws and extra-powerful front legs.

SCARY SKILLS: Rears up on its hind legs to knock victims down.

HOW SCARY?

SLOTH BEAR

3

LENGTH: 5–7 feet (1.5–2 m)

DEADLY WEAPONS: Extremely long, sharp front claws.

SCARY SKILLS: May strike at victims' faces or heads. Ouch!

HOW SCARY?

POLAR BEAR

2

LENGTH: 7–10 feet (2–3 m)

DEADLY WEAPONS: Very big and strong head, mouth, and teeth.

SCARY SKILLS: Can sniff out prey over long distances or through deep snow.

HOW SCARY?

BROWN BEAR

Brown bears, including grizzlies and Kodiak bears, will come close to humans, hoping for food. If threatened, they can rear up and stand up to 10 feet (3 m) tall. In an attack, brown bears may maul victims with their huge claws and teeth.

LENGTH: 5–10 feet (1.5–3 m)

DEADLY WEAPONS: Long, strong claws and teeth, and mighty strength and power.

SCARY SKILLS: Uses its giant paws to swipe at enemies—a single blow can be deadly.

HOW SCARY?
▲▲▲▲▲

KILLER FACT ★

Bears do sometimes eat humans. In 1915, a huge bear attacked a Japanese village, devouring seven people and injuring more.

BIG CATS

Big cats are the ultimate fierce, scary carnivores. If one of these decides to take on a human, it would almost certainly win!

5

JAGUAR

LENGTH: 5–6 feet (1.5–1.8 m)

DEADLY WEAPONS: Powerful bite, strong enough to crush the skulls of prey.

SCARY SKILLS: Hides in trees to pounce from above.

HOW SCARY?

4

COUGAR

LENGTH: 3–5 feet (1–1.6 m)

DEADLY WEAPONS: Very long, strong back legs for pouncing.

SCARY SKILLS: Makes a loud, spooky, screaming sound.

HOW SCARY?

3

LEOPARD

LENGTH: 4.24–6.25 feet (1.3–1.9 m)

DEADLY WEAPONS: Big, heavy, powerful paws and claws.

SCARY SKILLS: Drags dead prey up into trees to hide it from other animals.

HOW SCARY?

2

LION

LENGTH: 4.5–5 feet (1.4–2 m)

DEADLY WEAPONS: Huge head with superlong canine teeth.

SCARY SKILLS: Females get together to bring down large prey.

HOW SCARY?

TIGER

All the big cats here can and do kill people, but the tiger is the most dangerous of all. It's the biggest big cat and the only one that, in some places, has been known to actually hunt humans.

LENGTH: 7–11 feet (2–3.3 m)

DEADLY WEAPONS: Huge jaws and mighty biting strength.

SCARY SKILLS: Can make giant leaps of up to 33 feet (10 m).

HOW SCARY?
▲▲▲▲▲

KILLER FACT ★

Tigers often sneak up on their prey from behind, so people wear face masks on the backs of their heads to try to scare them away!

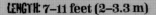

WOLVES, HYENAS, AND WILD DOGS

In fairy tales, wolves are evil villains that gobble people up in an instant. What are they really like?

5 JACKAL

LENGTH: 3–5 feet (0.9–1.5 m)

DEADLY WEAPONS: Long, pointed jaws.

SCARY SKILLS: High, wailing call.

HOW SCARY?

4 DINGO

LENGTH: 3–5 feet (0.9–1.5 m)

DEADLY WEAPONS: Broad head and long teeth.

SCARY SKILLS: Extremely fast runner.

HOW SCARY?

3 HYENA

LENGTH: 3–8 feet (1–1.9 m)

DEADLY WEAPONS: Superpowerful, bone-crushing jaw strength.

SCARY SKILLS: Can gobble up large prey in minutes!

HOW SCARY?

2 PAINTED HUNTING DOG

LENGTH: 3–5 feet (0.9–1.5 m)

DEADLY WEAPONS: Powerful, tenacious bite.

SCARY SKILLS: Hunts in packs to kill animals up to ten times its own size.

HOW SCARY?

GRAY WOLF

The widely feared gray wolf is a big animal and an excellent hunter, especially when it hunts in a pack. Long ago, when gray wolves were much more widespread, attacks on humans were very common, and their fearsome reputation lives on today.

LENGTH: 3–5 feet (0.9–1.5 m)

DEADLY WEAPONS: Long legs, large teeth, and a big bite.

SCARY SKILLS: Will track and chase prey for many miles.

HOW SCARY?

KILLER FACT ★

All pet dogs are descendants of the gray wolf, and some of them can be very dangerous, too.

MUSTELIDS

This is a group of small but fierce meat-eating mammals. Some are known for being bad-tempered and aggressive.

5 WEASEL

LENGTH: 8–10 inches (20–25 cm)

DEADLY WEAPONS: Though tiny, its sharp teeth can deliver a serious bite.

SCARY SKILLS: Very fierce and bad-tempered.

HOW SCARY? ▲▲△△△

4 SKUNK

LENGTH: 2–3 feet (0.6–0.9 m)

DEADLY WEAPONS: Feared for its burning, stinging, and horrendously stinky spray, used as a defense.

SCARY SKILLS: Can squirt its smelly spray from up to 10 feet (3 m) away.

HOW SCARY? ▲▲▲△△

3 BADGER

LENGTH: 2–3 feet (0.6–0.9 m)

DEADLY WEAPONS: Big, strong front claws.

SCARY SKILLS: Will bite and swipe dangerously if cornered.

HOW SCARY? ▲▲▲△△

2 GIANT OTTER

LENGTH: 5–6 feet (1.5–1.8 m)

DEADLY WEAPONS: Large head and powerful bite.

SCARY SKILLS: Easily upset; can be very dangerous in captivity.

HOW SCARY? ▲▲▲▲△

WOLVERINE

The biggest mustelid, the wolverine, is one of the fiercest animals on the planet. It is not scared of any other animal, and will attack and kill prey much bigger than itself. Luckily, wolverines live in remote northern forests and rarely encounter humans.

LENGTH: 3–4 feet (0.9–1.2 m)

DEADLY WEAPONS: Large paws with long, sharp claws.

SCARY SKILLS: Extremely strong and tenacious.

HOW SCARY?

KILLER FACT

Mustelids have backward-pointing teeth at the backs of their mouths, which help them to tear off chunks of frozen prey.

HERBIVORES

These plant-munching mammals are among the most dangerous of all wild animals. They won't eat us up, but they might charge, trample, or stab a human who gets in their way.

5

GIRAFFE

HEIGHT: 13–18 feet (4–5.5 m) tall

DEADLY WEAPONS: Long legs and hard, sharp hooves.

SCARY SKILLS: Can kick hard enough to kill a lion!

HOW SCARY?
▲▲▲△△

4

CAPE BUFFALO

LENGTH: 7–12 feet (2–3.7 m)

DEADLY WEAPONS: Huge, wide, very sharp horns.

SCARY SKILLS: Charges and stabs enemies, especially hunters who try to shoot it.

HOW SCARY?
▲▲▲▲△

3

BLACK RHINOCEROS

LENGTH: 10–13 feet (3–4 m)

DEADLY WEAPONS: Pointed nose horn up to 3 feet (1 m) long.

SCARY SKILLS: Charges enemies at high speeds.

HOW SCARY?
▲▲▲▲△

2

AFRICAN ELEPHANT

LENGTH: 13–27 feet (4–8 m)

DEADLY WEAPONS: Its weight, size, and long, sharp tusks.

SCARY SKILLS: Kills by charging, trampling, and crushing.

HOW SCARY?
▲▲▲▲▲

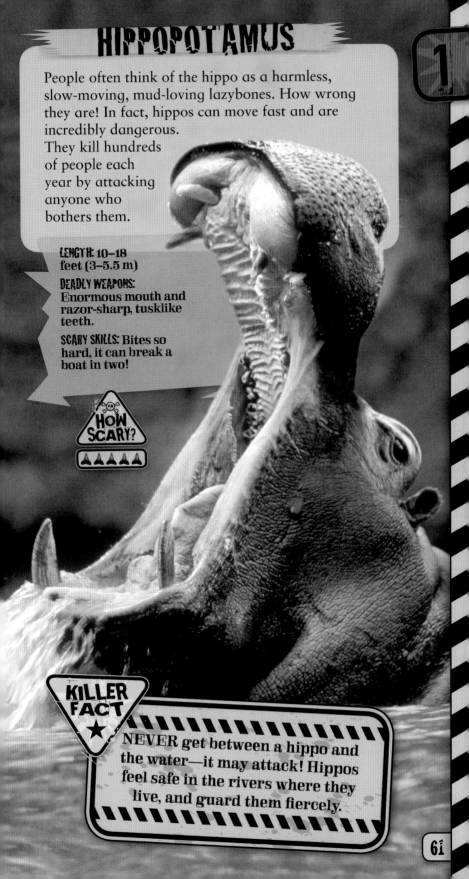

HIPPOPOTAMUS

People often think of the hippo as a harmless, slow-moving, mud-loving lazybones. How wrong they are! In fact, hippos can move fast and are incredibly dangerous. They kill hundreds of people each year by attacking anyone who bothers them.

LENGTH: 10–18 feet (3–5.5 m)

DEADLY WEAPONS: Enormous mouth and razor-sharp, tusklike teeth.

SCARY SKILLS: Bites so hard, it can break a boat in two!

HOW SCARY?
▲▲▲▲▲

KILLER FACT
★

NEVER get between a hippo and the water—it may attack! Hippos feel safe in the rivers where they live, and guard them fiercely.

SURPRISINGLY SCARY MAMMALS

Some scary mammals are really quite small, and even cute or friendly looking. Don't be fooled—always be careful around pigs, and don't ever think a chimp will make a good pet!

5 TASMANIAN DEVIL

LENGTH: 2–4 feet (0.6–1.2 m)

DEADLY WEAPONS: Incredibly strong bite for its size.

SCARY SKILLS: Makes a bloodcurdling, screeching sound.

HOW SCARY?

4 VAMPIRE BAT

LENGTH: 3–4 inches (8–10 cm)

DEADLY WEAPONS: Teeth so sharp, you can't feel them bite you!

SCARY SKILLS: Known for biting and slurping the blood of its prey.

HOW SCARY?

3 RED KANGAROO

HEIGHT: 4–7 feet (1.2–2.1 m)

DEADLY WEAPONS: Males have massive arm and chest muscles.

SCARY SKILLS: Fights viciously by kicking and "boxing" with its arms.

HOW SCARY?

2 WILD BOAR

LENGTH: 3–9 feet (1–2.7 m)

DEADLY WEAPONS: Four very sharp tusks.

SCARY SKILLS: Slashes upward with tusks, slicing into enemies.

HOW SCARY?

CHIMPANZEE

Chimpanzees may look cute, but they have a violent side, too. Both pet chimps and wild ones have attacked humans.

HEIGHT: 3–5 feet (1–1.5 m)

DEADLY WEAPONS: Very big, powerful arms and hands.

SCARY SKILLS: Attacks by biting and tearing at its enemies.

HOW SCARY?

KILLER FACT

Experts think that wild chimps may attack humans when they intrude onto the chimps' territory.

VULTURES

Vultures have a reputation for stalking dying animals, then swooping down to scavenge their dead bodies. Vultures do feed on dead animals, but are they dangerous to humans?

5 TURKEY VULTURE

LENGTH: 2–3 feet (0.6–0.9 cm)

DEADLY WEAPONS: Sharp, hooked beak for tearing the meat off dead animals.

SCARY SKILLS: Looks a bit scary, but rarely bothers humans.

HOW SCARY?

4 ANDEAN CONDOR

LENGTH: 3–4.5 feet (0.9–1.4 m)

DEADLY WEAPONS: Huge; capable of launching a savage attack, but avoids humans.

SCARY SKILLS: 10-foot (3 m) wingspan makes it good at swoooping down from the sky.

HOW SCARY?

3 BLACK VULTURE

LENGTH: 2–2.5 feet (0.6–0.8 m)

DEADLY WEAPONS: Sharp beak, used to peck out the eyes of its prey. Ouch!

SCARY SKILLS: Attacks in flocks to kill young cattle.

HOW SCARY?

2 GRIFFON VULTURE

LENGTH: 3–4 feet (0.9–1.2 m)

DEADLY WEAPONS: Big and strong; very sharp claws.

SCARY SKILLS: Excellent eyesight—can spot dead animals from high in the air.

HOW SCARY?

LAMMERGEIER

The lammergeier, also called the bearded vulture, is a powerful animal that hunts prey as well as feeding on carrion (dead animals). It sometimes swoops at mountain animals, such as goats, to force them over cliff edges, and may attack people in this way, too.

LENGTH: 3–4 feet (0.9–1.2 m)

DEADLY WEAPONS: Large, powerful body, beak, and claws.

SCARY SKILLS: Drops bones onto rocks from high in the sky, to smash them open and eat the bone marrow.

HOW SCARY?

KILLER FACT

Lammergeiers sometimes kill tortoises by smashing them onto rocks, as they do with bones.

1

EAGLES

Eagles are very large, powerful birds of prey and, unlike vultures, they mainly hunt and kill living animals. Eagle attacks on humans are rare, but not unheard of.

PHILIPPINE EAGLE

5

LENGTH: 36–45 inches (90–100 cm)

DEADLY WEAPONS: One of the biggest beaks of any eagle at up to 3 inches (7.6 cm) long.

SCARY SKILLS: Hunts in pairs—one eagle distracts some monkeys, while the other sneaks up on them.

HOW SCARY?

WEDGE-TAILED EAGLE

4

LENGTH: 32–40 inches (81–102 cm)

DEADLY WEAPONS: Very large and powerful.

SCARY SKILLS: Hunts in groups to kill animals as large as kangaroos.

HOW SCARY?

HARPY EAGLE

3

LENGTH: 35–40 inches (89–102 cm)

DEADLY WEAPONS: Huge talons as big as bears' paws.

SCARY SKILLS: Can carry off prey almost as heavy as itself, such as sloths, deer, and pigs.

HOW SCARY?

GOLDEN EAGLE

2

LENGTH: 32–38 inches (81–97 cm)

DEADLY WEAPONS: Very large, strong, sharp beak.

SCARY SKILLS: Kills large prey, such as deer and even bear cubs. Has also attacked people.

HOW SCARY?

WHITE-TAILED SEA EAGLE

The huge and powerful white-tailed sea eagle is probably the scariest of all the eagles. As its name suggests, it mainly catches fish, but its massive strength means it can also grab and carry away quite big animals such as lambs and small deer.

LENGTH: 32–38 inches (81–97 cm)

DEADLY WEAPONS: Massively strong talons that can carry huge weights.

SCARY SKILLS: Swoops and grabs victims from behind.

HOW SCARY?

KILLER FACT

In 1932, a white-tailed sea eagle reportedly carried off a three-year-old girl from her yard to its nest. She was later rescued alive. Phew!

OWLS

Owls are quiet, fluffy-feathered night birds, normally associated with hooting spookily. But get too close to their nests and they may attack and cause serious injury.

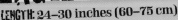

5 EAGLE OWL

LENGTH: 24–30 inches (60–75 cm)

DEADLY WEAPONS: Huge owl with a hooked, eaglelike beak.

SCARY SKILLS: Can catch large prey, such as hares and geese.

HOW SCARY?

4 GREAT HORNED OWL

LENGTH: 18–27 inches (46–69 cm)

DEADLY WEAPONS: Very sharp talons.

SCARY SKILLS: Said to have attacked people wearing pom-pom hats. Perhaps it mistook the pompoms for mice or voles!

HOW SCARY?

3 BARRED OWL

LENGTH: 18–20 inches (46–51 cm)

DEADLY WEAPONS: Strong, muscular build.

SCARY SKILLS: Has a habit of attacking people who pass its nesting areas.

HOW SCARY?

2 POWERFUL OWL

LENGTH: 18–27 inches (46–69 cm)

DEADLY WEAPONS: Very large feet with long talons.

SCARY SKILLS: Males may attack people who come near their nests, clawing at the head and face.

HOW SCARY?

TAWNY OWL

This owl is only medium-size, but is known to launch vicious attacks on anyone who bothers it or, even worse, its chicks. It aims for the head and has been known to tear people's faces to shreds.

LENGTH: 14–18 inches (35–45 cm)

DEADLY WEAPONS: Small, but stocky and strong, with sharp claws.

SCARY SKILLS: Flies silently, attacking victims unawares.

HOW SCARY?

KILLER FACT

In 1937, famous bird photographer Eric Hosking lost his left eye to a tawny owl during a photo shoot.

RAPTORS

The raptors, or birds of prey, are fierce hunting birds that are built to kill. Their weapons are razor-sharp beaks and claws, great eyesight, and superspeedy swooping skills.

5 RED KITE

HOW SCARY? ▲▲△△△

LENGTH: 24–26 inches (61–66 cm)

DEADLY WEAPONS: Very sharp, hooked beak.

SCARY SKILLS: Swoops down to snatch food from lunch boxes, and has been known to attack pet dogs.

4 PEREGRINE FALCON

HOW SCARY? ▲▲▲△△

LENGTH: 14–24 inches (35–60 cm)

DEADLY WEAPONS: Very strong legs and feet.

SCARY SKILLS: Can zoom down from the sky at 200 miles per hour (320 km/h).

3 HARRIS'S HAWK

LENGTH: 18–30 inches (45–75 cm)

DEADLY WEAPONS: Big, strong, and very sharp beak.

HOW SCARY? ▲▲▲▲△

SCARY SKILLS: Swoops suddenly; has attacked children.

2 BUZZARD

LENGTH: 18–22 inches (45–55 cm)

DEADLY WEAPONS: Very strong for its size.

HOW SCARY? ▲▲▲▲△

SCARY SKILLS: Targets its enemies by aiming for the head.

MISSISSIPPI KITE

Though quite small birds of prey, Mississippi kites can launch one of the scariest attacks. They get together into big flocks to dive-bomb anyone who strays close to their nesting sites. As the kites often nest in towns and cities, this can cause trouble!

LENGTH: 13–15 inches (33–38 cm)

DEADLY WEAPONS: Small but sharp beak.

SCARY SKILLS: High-speed, targeted dive-bombing.

HOW SCARY?
▲▲▲▲▲

KILLER FACT
★

Mississippi kites sometimes cause car accidents by dive-bombing cars, making them swerve and crash.

FLIGHTLESS AND POISONOUS BIRDS

They may not be able to get off the ground, but flightless birds are the fiercest ones of all. Their scariness is matched only by the world's few poisonous birds.

5

GREATER RHEA

HEIGHT: 4–4.7 feet (1.2–1.4 m)

DEADLY WEAPONS: Sturdy beak used to peck and jab enemies.

SCARY SKILLS: Makes a roaring, growling sound like a bear.

HOW SCARY?

4

EMU

HEIGHT: 5–7 feet (1.5–2.1 m)

DEADLY WEAPONS: Incredibly strong legs and claws.

SCARY SKILLS: Good at running fast and kicking hard.

HOW SCARY?

3

BLUE-CAPPED IFRIT

LENGTH: 6–7 inches (10–18 cm)

DEADLY WEAPONS: Skin and feathers contain a deadly poison, similar to that found on poison dart frogs.

SCARY SKILLS: Experts think they collect the poison from the beetles they eat.

HOW SCARY?

2

CASSOWARY

HEIGHT: 5–7 feet (1.5–2.1 m)

DEADLY WEAPONS: Huge, sharp killer middle claw on each foot.

SCARY SKILLS: Kicks hard enough to tear an animal open or rip through a car door.

HOW SCARY?

OSTRICH

The ostrich is the biggest, heaviest, and fastest-running bird in the world. When they're annoyed, ostriches chase people and even cars. They can easily kill a human with a single kick.

HEIGHT: 6–9 feet (1.8–2.7 m)

DEADLY WEAPONS: Huge, powerful legs and claws.

SCARY SKILLS: Top running speed of 45 miles per hour (72 km/h).

HOW SCARY?

KILLER FACT

Ostriches are pretty useful to us. Their feathers make dusters, their skin is used as leather, and some people eat their meat for dinner!

WATERBIRDS

Swans, geese, and seagulls are a familiar sight to many people, but they can be fierce. Geese are sometimes used instead of guard dogs!

5

CANADA GOOSE

LENGTH: 32–44 inches (80–110 cm)

DEADLY WEAPONS: Huge wings, up to 6 feet (1.8 m) across.

SCARY SKILLS: Spreads its wings, hisses, then charges at enemies.

HOW SCARY?

4

GREAT SKUA

LENGTH: 20–24 inches (50–60 cm)

DEADLY WEAPONS: Sharp, hooked beak.

SCARY SKILLS: Fierce and fearless; attacks anyone near its nest.

HOW SCARY?

3

GANNET

LENGTH: 34–42 inches (86–107 cm)

DEADLY WEAPONS: Thick, strong beak, which can peck people's eyes out.

SCARY SKILLS: Folds its wings and plunges into the sea at high speed—don't get in the way!

HOW SCARY?

2

HERRING GULL

LENGTH: 22–28 inches (55–70 cm)

DEADLY WEAPONS: Strong wings and big, tough beak.

SCARY SKILLS: Dive-bombs people during its breeding season.

HOW SCARY?

MUTE SWAN

Swans may be beautiful and peaceful, but they are very BIG. When a swan decides to defend its nest or chicks, it will attack with its huge wings and beak. A swan attack can break a person's arm or leg, and some attacks have even resulted in people drowning.

LENGTH: 4.5–6 feet (1.4–1.8 m)

DEADLY WEAPONS: Powerful wings containing bony knobs used as weapons.

SCARY SKILLS: Thrashing with its wings hard enough to break human arms or legs.

HOW SCARY?

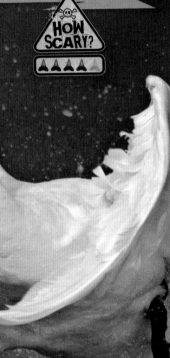

KILLER FACT

Swans sometimes attack people in kayaks and canoes, especially when the swans are building their nests.

ANTS

Like humans, ants work together to build a home and grow or collect food. To help them defend their colony against enemies, most ants can both bite and sting.

5

MARICOPA HARVESTER ANT

LENGTH: 0.75–1 inch (18–25 mm)

DEADLY WEAPONS: Most toxic venom of any insect.

SCARY SKILLS: Horribly painful sting, though not usually deadly, as there is very little venom.

HOW SCARY?

4

BULLET ANT

LENGTH: 0.75–1 inch (18–25 mm)

DEADLY WEAPONS: Most painful insect sting.

SCARY SKILLS: Makes a beeping noise and releases a stinky smell before going on the attack.

HOW SCARY?

3

FIRE ANT

LENGTH: 0.25 inch (6 mm)

DEADLY WEAPONS: Painful, burning sting that can be deadly if many ants attack at once.

SCARY SKILLS: When one fire ant stings, the others sense it and rush to attack.

HOW SCARY?

2

ARMY ANT

LENGTH: 0.5 inch (13 mm)

DEADLY WEAPONS: Large jaws and a powerful, painful bite.

SCARY SKILLS: Goes on the rampage in swarms of up to 20 million, eating every animal in its path.

HOW SCARY?

BULLDOG ANT

This is one of the biggest and most aggressive ants in the world. A bulldog ant will attack a human and its sting, though rarely deadly, is very painful.

LENGTH: 0.5–1.6 inches (12–40 mm)

DEADLY WEAPONS: Extremely powerful, painful sting.

SCARY SKILLS: Excellent eyesight—it looks out for enemies, then chases them.

HOW SCARY?
▲▲▲▲▲

KILLER FACT ★

Bulldog ants use their massive jaws to grab and slice up their prey—other insects.

BEES

Besides making honey, bees pollinate plants, helping us grow flowers, fruit, and vegetables. However, they do (usually) have a nasty stinger.

5

BUMBLEBEE

LENGTH: 0.5–1.3 inch (10.5–20.5 cm)

DEADLY WEAPONS: Females have a stinger, but it's not too serious.

SCARY SKILLS: Bumblebees can make people panic, as they're often very large.

HOW SCARY?

4

TROPICAL CARPENTER BEE

LENGTH: About 1.5 inches (3.8 cm)

DEADLY WEAPONS: Has a stinger, but uses it rarely.

SCARY SKILLS: Huge, terrifying-looking bee, though actually not very dangerous.

HOW SCARY?

3

STINGLESS BEE

LENGTH: 0.25 inch or less (0.6 cm)

DEADLY WEAPONS: Stinger is tiny, so it has a powerful bite instead.

SCARY SKILLS: Releases chemicals from its head that can make a victim's skin blister.

HOW SCARY?

2

HONEYBEE

LENGTH: 0.25–0.75 inch (0.6–1.9 cm)

DEADLY WEAPONS: Painful sting that can sometimes cause allergies and even be fatal.

SCARY SKILLS: Each bee will give its life to save the colony.

HOW SCARY?

KILLER BEE

These bees are a type of honeybee accidentally released by scientists. Their sting is no worse than any other honeybees', but they are much more aggressive and likely to attack in a large swarm—so victims can get stung hundreds of times.

LENGTH: 0.25–0.5 inch (0.6–1.9 cm)

DEADLY WEAPONS: Stings just like a normal honeybee.

SCARY SKILLS: Will swarm, chase, and attack anyone who annoys them.

HOW SCARY?

KILLER FACT ★

Hiding underwater will not deter killer bees. They will wait for you to come back up to breathe!

WASPS

Wasps are related to bees, and are known for being more aggressive and more likely to sting than their cousins. Some of them look superscary, too.

GIANT HORNTAIL

5

LENGTH: 1–1.5 inches (20.5–3.8 cm)

DEADLY WEAPONS: Strong jaws for biting through wood.

SCARY SKILLS: Has what looks like an enormous, scary stinger, but it's actually just used for laying eggs.

HOW SCARY?

COMMON WASP

4

LENGTH: 0.5–0.75 inch (0.6–1.9 cm)

DEADLY WEAPONS: Stinger that can be reused many times.

SCARY SKILLS: Aggressive and will attack in a swarm.

HOW SCARY?

BALD-FACED HORNET

3

LENGTH: 0.5–0.75 inch (0.6–1.9 cm)

DEADLY WEAPONS: Painful sting that can be dangerous.

SCARY SKILLS: Gets very angry if its large nest is disturbed.

HOW SCARY?

TARANTULA HAWK WASP

2

LENGTH: 1.5–2 inches (3.8–5 cm)

DEADLY WEAPONS: Extremely painful sting that can leave victims helpless for a while.

SCARY SKILLS: Stings a tarantula and lays its eggs inside it, so the wasp's larvae can feed on the living tarantula.

HOW SCARY?

ASIAN GIANT HORNET

Imagine this humongous creature landing on your lunch! This is one of the world's biggest wasps, and it IS as scary as it looks—in Asia, several people die every year from giant hornet stings, especially those unlucky victims who get stung several times.

LENGTH: 1.5–2 inches (3.8–5 cm)

DEADLY WEAPONS: Very long stinger that injects a large dose of killer venom.

SCARY SKILLS: Uses its big jaws to slice off honeybees' heads.

HOW SCARY?

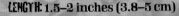

KILLER FACT

The Asian giant hornet's sting is said to feel like being stabbed with a hot nail. Yikes!

FLIES

They hang around dead bodies and garbage bins, and their eggs hatch into maggots. Some can give us nasty bites and suck our blood. But worse are the diseases flies spread.

5

HOUSEFLY

LENGTH: 0.25 inch or less (6 mm)

DEADLY WEAPONS: Long, strawlike mouth for dissolving and sucking up food.

SCARY SKILLS: Dribbles and poops constantly, spreading germs onto human foods.

HOW SCARY?

4

HORSE FLY

LENGTH: 0.75 inch or less (19 mm)

DEADLY WEAPONS: Sharp jaws that stab or slice into skin.

SCARY SKILLS: Sucks blood and spreads diseases between animals and people.

HOW SCARY?

3

SAND FLY

LENGTH: Tinier than even 0.25 inch (6 mm)

DEADLY WEAPONS: Sharp, bloodsucking mouthparts

SCARY SKILLS: Spreads leishmaniasis, a deadly disease that makes large sores on the body.

HOW SCARY?

2

T'SET'SE FLY

LENGTH: 0.5 inch or less (13 mm)

DEADLY WEAPONS: Razor-sharp, bladelike mouthparts.

SCARY SKILLS: Spreads sleeping sickness, a horrible disease that causes tiredness, confusion, and death.

HOW SCARY?

MOSQUITO

These tiny insects may not look scary, but mosquitoes are by far the deadliest animals in this book. They carry and spread germs that cause diseases such as yellow fever, West Nile virus, and malaria, which kill millions of people every year.

LENGTH: Less than 0.25 inch (19 mm)

DEADLY WEAPONS: Long, needlelike sucking mouthparts.

SCARY SKILLS: Spreads several extremely deadly diseases.

HOW SCARY?
▲▲▲▲▲

KILLER FACT ★

Mosquitoes have caused more human deaths than all the wars in history.

BEETLES

There are over 350,000 species of beetles, many more than there are of any other animal. Most are harmless, but there are a few you might want to avoid. . . .

5

BOMBARDIER BEETLE

LENGTH: Up to about 1 inch (25 mm)

DEADLY WEAPONS: Special chamber in abdomen for mixing explosive chemicals.

SCARY SKILLS: Attacks enemies by blasting hot, smelly, stinging gases out of its rear end!

HOW SCARY?
▲▲▲▲▲

4

ROVE BEETLE

LENGTH: 0.25 inch or less (6 mm)

DEADLY WEAPONS: Releases a chemical that leaves a painful rash.

SCARY SKILLS: Causes mysterious, sudden outbreaks of skin rash.

HOW SCARY?
▲▲▲▲▲

3

DOMINO BEETLE

LENGTH: 1.5–2.5 inches (4–6 cm)

DEADLY WEAPONS: Squirts a jet of painful acid to scare away predators.

SCARY SKILLS: Gives off a revolting smell.

HOW SCARY?
▲▲▲▲▲

2

SPANISH FLY

LENGTH: 0.25–1 inch (6–24 mm)

DEADLY WEAPONS: Releases a deadly poisonous chemical that stings and blisters the skin.

SCARY SKILLS: Often hides in hay and gets eaten by farm animals, with deadly results.

HOW SCARY?
▲▲▲▲▲

TITAN BEETLE

This is probably the beetle that could give you the biggest fright! It is MASSIVE and makes a noise like a helicopter as it flies through the air. Its powerful jaws are strong enough to bite through a pencil, but luckily these monsters mostly leave humans alone.

LENGTH: Up to 6.5 inches (16.5 cm)

DEADLY WEAPONS: Superstrong, pincerlike biting jaws.

SCARY SKILLS: Attacks enemies with sharp spines on its legs.

HOW SCARY?

KILLER FACT

After becoming adults from wood-eating larvae, titan beetles do not feed and live for only a few weeks.

BUGS

The word *bugs* is used to describe all kinds of creepy crawlies and even germs. But bugs are also a particular order of insects, some of which are superscary!

5

BEDBUG

LENGTH: Less than 0.25 inch (0.6 cm)

DEADLY WEAPONS: Stabbing mouthparts used to suck your blood.

SCARY SKILLS: Hides in cracks and crevices, then sneaks out at night to bite you.

HOW SCARY?

4

WHEEL BUG

LENGTH: About 1 inch (2.5 cm)

DEADLY WEAPONS: Thick, curved "beak" that injects poison, giving a painful bite.

SCARY SKILLS: Stabs its prey, then dissolves its insides and slurps them up!

HOW SCARY?

3

BACKSWIMMER

LENGTH: About 0.25 inch (0.6 cm)

DEADLY WEAPONS: Powerful and agonizing stabbing bite.

SCARY SKILLS: Uses its long, oar-shaped legs to swim fast on its back.

HOW SCARY?

2

GIANT WATER BUG

LENGTH: 4–5 inches (10–13 cm)

DEADLY WEAPONS: Huge, with a horribly painful bite.

SCARY SKILLS: Can move fast by swimming, running, or flying.

HOW SCARY?

KISSING BUG

This bug's name makes it sound friendly, but the name actually comes from the bug's habit of biting people around the eyes or mouth as they sleep. Kissing bugs carry and spread a horrible illness, Chagas' disease, which can be deadly.

LENGTH: 0.75–0.25 inches (1.9–3.2 cm)

DEADLY WEAPONS: Spreads disease as it sucks your blood.

SCARY SKILLS: Creeps up the body to bite you on the face. Gross!

HOW SCARY?

▲▲▲▲▲

KILLER FACT ★

Naturalist Charles Darwin described kissing bugs as "most disgusting" after he was bitten by them.

MORE SCARY INSECTS

Besides bees, beetles, bugs, and flies, there are all kinds of other insects that it might be a good idea to stay away from....

OAK PROCESSIONARY MOTH

5

LENGTH: About 1 inch (2–2.5 cm)

DEADLY WEAPONS: Caterpillars are covered in thousands of poisonous hairs.

SCARY SKILLS: The hairs break off and cause skin rashes and asthma.

HOW SCARY? ▲▲▲△△

COCKROACH

4

LENGTH: 1.25–2 inches (3–5 cm)

DEADLY WEAPONS: Spreads germs, is smelly, and its poop can cause allergies.

SCARY SKILLS: Incredibly fast runner.

HOW SCARY? ▲▲▲▲△

TWO-STRIPED WALKING STICK

3

LENGTH: 1.5–3 inches (3.8–7.6 cm)

DEADLY WEAPONS: Squirts a strong chemical spray at enemies.

SCARY SKILLS: If the spray gets in victims' eyes, it can blind them for a while.

HOW SCARY? ▲▲▲△△

TERMITES

2

LENGTH: 0.25 inch (0.6 cm)

DEADLY WEAPONS: Biting mouthparts for chewing wood.

SCARY SKILLS: Can cause wooden homes, bridges, and trees to collapse or fall down.

HOW SCARY? ▲▲▲▲△

LOCUSTS

Locusts are a type of grasshopper that sometimes get together in a big, hungry, plant-munching swarm. They don't bite or sting people but, by gobbling up huge areas of crops, they can cause famines that may kill thousands of people.

LENGTH: 3–3.5 inches (7.6–9 cm)

DEADLY WEAPONS: Munching mouths that strip plants bare.

SCARY SKILLS: Can form terrifying swarms of billions of hungry insects.

HOW SCARY?

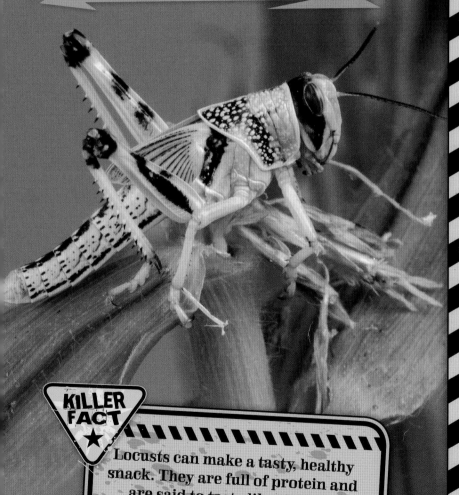

KILLER FACT

Locusts can make a tasty, healthy snack. They are full of protein and are said to taste like shrimp.

SPIDERS

Most people are naturally wary of spiders, and there's a good reason. There are quite a few species that are very dangerous to humans.

5 BROWN RECLUSE SPIDER

LENGTH: around 1 inch (2.5 cm) across

DEADLY WEAPONS: Nasty bite that can rot away skin and flesh.

SCARY SKILLS: Hides in old clothes and gloves.

HOW SCARY?
▲▲▲△△

4 COBALT BLUE TARANTULA

LENGTH: 4–6 inches (10–15 cm) across

DEADLY WEAPONS: Powerful bite and very grumpy attitude.

SCARY SKILLS: Moves quickly.

HOW SCARY?
▲▲▲▲△

3 REDBACK SPIDER

LENGTH: around 1.5 inches (3.8 cm) across

DEADLY WEAPONS: Very painful and dangerous bite.

SCARY SKILLS: Hides in piles of garbage and under toilet seats!

HOW SCARY?
▲▲▲▲▲

2 FUNNEL-WEB SPIDER

LENGTH: 2–3 inches (5–7.6 cm) across

DEADLY WEAPONS: Deadly bite that can stop a victim's breathing.

SCARY SKILLS: Waves its big black front legs when it's annoyed.

HOW SCARY?
▲▲▲▲△

BRAZILIAN WANDERING SPIDER

This scary spider is one of the most venomous in the world. It comes from South America, but sometimes gets shipped around the world in bunches of bananas. Imagine this monster jumping out of the fruit bowl!

LENGTH: 4–5 inches (10–12.7 cm) across

DEADLY WEAPONS: Killer venom that causes paralysis and suffocation.

SCARY SKILLS: Hides in bunches of bananas.

HOW SCARY?

KILLER FACT

They hide away by day, but at night, wandering spiders come out and . . . wander around.

SCORPIONS

A scorpion's weapons are big snapping pincers at its front, and a huge, curved, stinging tail at the back end. Not every scorpion is deadly, but these five species are all killers.

5 BLACK SPITTING THICKTAIL

LENGTH: 3.5–6 inches (9–15 cm)

DEADLY WEAPONS: Very thick tail with a sting that can be fatal.

SCARY SKILLS: Can squirt its venom into victims' eyes, causing blindness.

HOW SCARY?

4 ARABIAN FAT-TAILED SCORPION

LENGTH: 3–4 inches (7.6–10 cm)

DEADLY WEAPONS: Powerful, sometimes lethal venom.

SCARY SKILLS: Often hides inside houses.

HOW SCARY?

3 YELLOW FAT-TAILED SCORPION

LENGTH: 3–4 inches (8–10 cm)

DEADLY WEAPONS: Fat tail full of deadly venom AND big, strong pincers.

SCARY SKILLS: Amazingly tough; able to survive desert sandstorms unharmed.

HOW SCARY?

2 DEATHSTALKER

LENGTH: 1.5–3.5 inches (3.8–9 cm)

DEADLY WEAPONS: Agonizingly painful and dangerous sting.

SCARY SKILLS: Looks similar to some less dangerous scorpions—watch out!

HOW SCARY?

INDIAN RED SCORPION

This supremely scary scorpion causes deaths every year in India and Nepal. Though it prefers to live in farmland and fields, it does go into houses. Then it sometimes drops down on people's beds from the ceiling during the night. Yikes!

LENGTH: 2–3.5 inches (5–9 cm)

DEADLY WEAPONS: Small, but has an extremely deadly sting.

SCARY SKILLS: Good at crawling across ceilings.

HOW SCARY?
▲▲▲▲▲

KILLER FACT ★

Scorpions love hiding away in dark, cozy places. So you should always check shoes and sleeping bags when in scorpion territory!

CREEPY CRAWLIES

Slimy, wriggling, or many-legged creatures can be scary.
Most of them are pretty small and harmless, but some
are quite large and can give you a nasty bite!

5

CHIGGER

HOW SCARY?

LENGTH: Tiny fraction of an inch (1–2 mm)

DEADLY WEAPONS: Sharp jaws for latching onto your skin.

SCARY SKILLS: Dissolves skin cells and sucks up the juice.

4

WHIP SCORPION

LENGTH: 4–6 inches (10–15 cm), including the long "whip" tail

DEADLY WEAPONS: Powerful claws that can give a painful pinch.

SCARY SKILLS: Also sprays acid that stings the eyes.

HOW SCARY?

3

HOW SCARY?

GIANT AFRICAN MILLIPEDE

LENGTH: 10–11 inches (25–28 cm)

DEADLY WEAPONS: Releases a chemical that stings skin and can damage eyes.

SCARY SKILLS: Rolls up into a hard, shiny ball to avoid danger.

2

GIANT CAMEL SPIDER

LENGTH: Up to 6 inches (15 cm)

DEADLY WEAPONS: Sharp, pincerlike jaws that can bite through skin.

HOW SCARY?

SCARY SKILLS: Terrifying to look at and can run scarily fast!

PERUVIAN GIANT CENTIPEDE

Centipedes are fierce hunters that inject venom into their prey. Small ones can't hurt humans, but this monster's bite is venomous enough to cause extreme pain and fever in the unlucky victim.

LENGTH: 8–12 inches (20–30 cm)

DEADLY WEAPONS: Sharp, venom-injecting claws on head.

SCARY SKILLS: Runs and climbs quickly with its big, strong legs.

HOW SCARY?
▲▲▲▲

KILLER FACT

As they hang from the ceilings of caves, these massive centipedes catch bats for dinner.

PARASITES

Parasites are creatures that depend on another animal to survive. Human parasites can live on or inside our bodies, helping themselves to our food or eating our body parts!

5

LIVER FLUKE

LENGTH: 1.2–2.75 inches (3–7 cm)

DEADLY WEAPONS: Powerful sucking mouth for feeding on your liver.

SCARY SKILLS: Gets into the body in raw river fish, or on water plants like watercress.

HOW SCARY?

4

HORSE BOTFLY

LENGTH: 0.6–0.7 inches (15–1.9 cm)

DEADLY WEAPONS: Its maggots bury themselves in horses' tongues or gums, or sometimes human skin!

SCARY SKILLS: Can zoom around over long distances to track down an unlucky host.

HOW SCARY?

3

GUINEA WORM

LENGTH: Up to 3 feet (0.9 m)

DEADLY WEAPONS: Uses a shrimplike water animal as a way to get inside people's stomachs.

SCARY SKILLS: Burrows from the stomach to the leg or foot, then wriggles out, causing intense pain.

HOW SCARY?

2

TAPEWORM

LENGTH: Up to 50 feet (15 m)

DEADLY WEAPONS: Hooklike mouth for hanging on to the inside of intestines.

SCARY SKILLS: Can grow to huge lengths inside you as it feeds on all that you eat.

HOW SCARY?

HOOKWORM

Hookworms are tiny, but they are killer parasites. They get into the human body through the skin and travel to the intestines. There, they live by feeding on vitims' blood, making the victims horribly ill.

LENGTH: 0.5 inch or less (5–13 mm)

DEADLY WEAPONS: Hangs on to the intestine wall with sharp teeth.

SCARY SKILLS: Sucks blood from the intestines.

HOW SCARY?

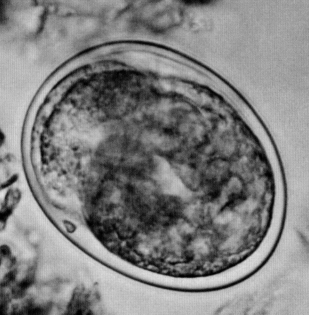

KILLER FACT

Around 50,000 people die every year from diseases caused by hookworm infection.

BLOODSUCKERS

Beasts like leeches and fleas live by sucking the blood of mammals, including humans. That's pretty scary, but to make matters worse, they can spread deadly germs, too.

5

HOW SCARY?
▲▲▲△△

TIGER LEECH

LENGTH: 2–5 inches (5–10 cm)

DEADLY WEAPONS: Long, needlelike mouthpart, or proboscis, for injecting into the skin to suck blood.

SCARY SKILLS: Detects movement in water and swims toward it.

4

LAMPREY

LENGTH: 18–36 inches (45–90 cm)

DEADLY WEAPONS: Dozens of teeth and a sharp tongue.

SCARY SKILLS: Attaches to larger fish, humans, or other victims, and munches into their flesh.

HOW SCARY?
▲▲▲△△

3

HOW SCARY?
▲▲▲▲△

TICK

LENGTH: Up to 1.2 inches (3 cm)

DEADLY WEAPONS: Some types have a needlelike mouth or fangs for sucking blood.

SCARY SKILLS: Can spread serious diseases such as Lyme disease.

2

BODY LOUSE

LENGTH: Tiny fraction of an inch (2–3.5 mm)

DEADLY WEAPONS: Sharp mouthparts for piercing skin and sucking blood.

SCARY SKILLS: Hides in seams of clothing, and can spread deadly diseases like typhus.

HOW SCARY?
▲▲▲▲△

FLEA

Fleas live on pets and other animals, but they bite humans, too. They suck your blood and leave an itchy sore. Fleas have supertough, hard bodies that are almost impossible to squash. Mostly, fleas are just a nuisance—but they can carry diseases.

LENGTH: Tiny fraction of an inch (1–10 mm)

DEADLY WEAPONS: Dagger-shaped mouthparts for jabbing into skin.

SCARY SKILLS: Amazing jumping ability for leaping onto a new host.

HOW SCARY?

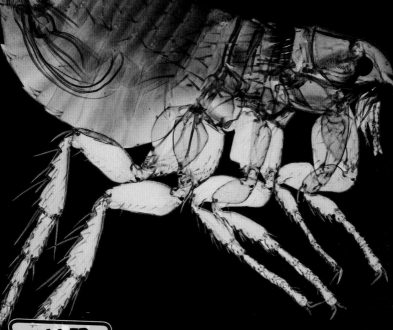

KILLER FACT

Rat fleas may have been responsible for spreading bubonic plague, which killed at least 75 million people.

THE TOP 100

If you've read this far, you'll know all about the different types of fearsome animals. But which are the scariest of the scariest? Check out this countdown to the most fearsome creature in the entire world!

Tawny Owl
A big owl native to Asia and Europe, it uses its sharp claws to tear at anyone who comes too close to its nest.

Tick
Ticks latch on to the skin of animals or humans to suck blood—sometimes spreading disease.

Termites
These cockroach-like insects live in warmer parts of the world. They feed on wood and can damage buildings.

Mississippi Kite
This small bird of prey from the US causes trouble by swooping and attacking people and cars in cities.

Sand Fly
A small, tropical fly that has caused hundreds of deaths in India by spreading a killer disease.

White-Tailed Sea Eagle
Massive European and Asian bird of prey, big enough to carry away a baby or young child.

Mute Swan
This beautiful, large waterbird can attack dangerously to defend its nest.

Ostrich
Fast-running, tall, and strong, this flightless African bird is the world's biggest bird, with a killer kick.

Body Louse
Bloodsucking lice that live on your body and can, in certain circumstances, spread serious diseases.

Cane Toad
This large toad is covered in a yucky slime that is deadly poisonous to many animals.

Lammergeier
A powerful vulture of Europe, Asia, and Africa, it may attack living animals—including humans.

Sperm Whale
This huge, voracious hunting whale can fight back fiercely if attacked by humans.

Southern Elephant Seal
Enormous, fearsomely strong seal that could easily flatten a human, but usually chooses other elephant seals.

Great Hammerhead
A large coastal shark with a weird, scarily shaped head, the great hammerhead really is a fearsome fish.

Sea Cucumber
These blobby-looking sea creatures have a secret weapon—dangerous gloop that can cause blindness.

Blue Sea Slug
This bizarre-looking blue sea creature, found worldwide, is tiny but has a very painful sting.

Titan Beetle
Scary looking but mild-mannered, this massive beetle from South America has a big bite.

Inland Taipan
Though one of the world's most venomous snakes, the inland taipan is so shy that it rarely bothers humans.

Hyena
Asian and African doglike animal that is tough and fierce, with a very powerful bite.

Blue Marlin
This huge and very fast sea fish has a huge spike on its snout. It will fight anyone who tries to catch it.

Killer Whale
Despite its name, the killer whale, or orca, rarely attacks people, except in captivity, where it can be dangerous.

Army Ants
These ants form massive swarms in the African jungle, and running into them would definitely not be fun!

Cassowary
This incredibly fierce flightless bird from Australia and New Guinea has extremely strong, sharp claws.

Barracuda
Big silvery fish with sharp teeth, found in tropical seas, barracudas are fierce and can give you a horrible bite.

Leopard
The fearsome spotty leopard of Africa and Asia can become a deadly killer in some situations

Painted Hunting Dog
A supersmart wild African dog that is excellent at hunting in packs to bring down big prey.

Oceanic Whitetip Shark
A fierce, fast, ocean-swimming shark that may prey on corpses—or even survivors—from shipwrecks.

Humboldt Squid
Big, fast, and highly intelligent, this squid lives in the eastern Pacific, where it is feared by local people.

Stingray
Stingrays swim in tropical seas and rivers around the world, and can inflict a painful sting with their tail spines.

Cape Buffalo
A cowlike animal that's smarter than it looks, this African buffalo has been known to attack in revenge.

Lion
Lions are found in Africa. They are famously fierce, but actually are not as dangerous as tigers.

Olive Sea Snake
A venomous snake that lives around coral reefs in the Pacific and Indian oceans, but mostly avoids humans.

Common Krait
A dangerous snake of India. The krait's bite can be deadly if victims don't get treatment quickly.

Black Rhinoceros
Africa's large black rhino is a plant eater, but has a bad temper and may charge.

Blue Shark
A large, fast-swimming ocean shark, found worldwide, that has been known to attack and kill humans.

Tapeworm
A disgusting parasite that can live inside a person's guts for years, becoming meters long—yuck!

Rattlesnake
Found in the Americas, rattlesnakes are very venomous, although they bite only if provoked.

Forest Vine Snake
This African snake has extremely deadly venom, but luckily it doesn't often bite.

Black Spitting Thicktail
A scary scorpion from southern Africa that can both sting and spray venom with its tail.

Chimpanzee
This African ape is similar in size to a human, but much stronger and capable of deadly attacks.

Black Caiman
An extremely large South American crocodile-like reptile that considers humans a tasty treat.

African Rock Python
This constrictor is Africa's largest snake. Attacks on humans are rare but have been known.

Habu Jelly
A dangerous jellyfish found around Japan and parts of Asia. Similar to the killer box jellyfish, but smaller.

Puff Adder
A shy but very venomous snake from Africa, where lack of medical care can result in death from its bite.

Stokes' Sea Snake
This sea snake is very big and has huge fangs and a venomous bite, but rarely causes human deaths.

Mexican Beaded Lizard
A dangerous lizard found in and around Mexico, with a venomous bite that causes severe pain.

Tarantula Hawk Wasp
This huge and fearsome wasp from the Americas is not a killer, but its sting is incredibly painful.

Electric Eel
The South American river eel zaps enemies with its shock. It is the world's most powerful electric animal.

Killer Bee
An extra-dangerous breed of honeybee, killer bees often attack in a swarm and can sting people to death.

American Alligator
A very big, powerful predator found in the US, this alligator has a mighty bite and could easily eat a human.

Arabian Fat-Tailed Scorpion
50 One of many dangerous scorpions found in the Arabian Desert, with a thick tail for storing its powerful venom.

 ## Lionfish
49 Spiky, spiny, highly venomous fish of the Indian and Pacific oceans, whose sting is occasionally fatal.

 ## Sloth Bear
48 The slow-moving but very fierce and bad-tempered Indian bear that is known to attack humans.

 ## Funnel-Web Spider
47 A large, black Australian spider that spins a tubelike web and has a very serious, sometimes fatal bite.

 ## Boomslang
46 This big-eyed African snake has a deadly bite that victims may not feel at first.

 ## Redback Spider
45 From Australia, this spider can give a human an extremely painful bite.

 ## Giant Spitting Cobra
44 Large African cobra with a painful bite and the ability to spit venom that can cause blindness.

 ## Peruvian Giant Centipede
43 A fast-moving, multilegged monster that can deliver an extremely unpleasant venomous bite.

 ## Leopard Seal
42 This giant, fast, and fierce seal lives around Antarctica, where it preys mainly on penguins and other seals.

 ## Hookworm
41 They may be small and difficult to see, but hookworms wreak fearsome havoc inside the guts of their hosts.

 ## Locust
40 Locusts can cause starvation by swarming and devouring huge areas of crops.

 ## Flea
39 Fleas can spread bubonic plague, which can be treated easily today, but killed millions in the 1300s.

 ## Kissing Bug
38 This bloodsucking bug from South America bites victims on the face and spreads deadly Chagas' disease.

Tsetse Fly
A biting, blood-sucking African fly that spreads several fatal diseases, including sleeping sickness.

Mosquito
Tiny mosquitoes have a truly fearsome skill of spreading malaria and other deadly diseases.

Green Anaconda
The world's biggest snake, found in South America, can easily catch large prey, squeeze it to death, and swallow it.

Geographer Cone
Attacks are rare, but this sea snail, found in shallow, warm, tropical oceans, has a very serious sting.

Flower Urchin
The flower urchin is a slow-moving spiny sea creature with an agonizing and sometimes deadly sting.

Shortfin Mako
A fast and fierce shark found around the world, the shortfin mako can be a fearsome enemy.

Gray Wolf
With their scary howls, wolves can be really fearsome. They live in many of the colder parts of the world.

Bull Shark
A big, strong shark found in coastal waters, the bull shark also swims up rivers and is often responsible for attacks.

Polar Bear
The polar bear looks more cuddly than fearsome, but watch out—it is highly dangerous up close.

Goonch
The goonch is a huge and scary river catfish from Asia that may seek out human flesh to eat.

African Elephant
They are known as peaceful animals, but elephants are pretty fearsome—they kill hundreds of people each year.

Bulldog Ant
This very large and fearsome Australian ant has an unbearably painful and sometimes dangerous bite.

Tiger Shark
The huge tiger shark is a ravenous hunter found in tropical seas, known for devouring a wide range of prey.

Russell's Viper

24

A highly venomous viper found across Asia. It is one of the world's most common dangerous snakes.

Philippine Cobra

23

Only found in the islands of the Philippines, this is a large and very dangerous snake that can spit venom.

Wolverine

22

A strong, bold, fierce mammal from the forests of the far north, the wolverine can take on almost any foe.

Terciopelo

21

An unusually aggressive, large, venomous snake from South and Central America.

Nile Crocodile

20

Africa's largest croc is a mighty monster that can snap up anything in or around the rivers and lakes where it lives.

Asian Giant Hornet

19

This ginormous wasp from eastern Asia has a very painful and powerful sting that can even kill.

Yellow Fat-Tailed Scorpion

18

A deadly scorpion of North Africa, with an extra-thick tail packed with fearsome killer venom.

Reticulated Python

17

This snake of Southeast Asia is a huge, very long constrictor that has been known to eat humans.

Stonefish

16

The world's most venomous fish, the stonefish lives in the shallow waters of the Pacific and Indian oceans.

Golden Poison Dart Frog

15

One of the world's deadliest poisons is found on the slimy skin of this small, brightly colored South American frog.

Spectacled Cobra

14

This large Asian snake is equipped with a deadly bite, making it one of the most feared snakes on the planet.

Death Stalker

13

A small but deadly desert scorpion of North Africa and the Middle East, with very powerful venom.

Australian Box Jelly

12

This is one of the world's most venomous animals. Every year, people die from its stings.

Great White Shark
The most fearsome shark of all, the massive great white can easily gobble up human-size and even larger prey.

Beaked Sea Snake
This extremely venomous sea snake lives in the Indian and Pacific oceans. It is bad-tempered and often bites.

Indian Red Scorpion
Probably the most venomous of all scorpions, the Indian red is a much-feared killer in parts of Asia.

Hippopotamus
The river-loving, grass-munching African giant is a fearsome beast, which can kill by biting and trampling.

Tiger
The most fearsome of the big cats, the tiger lives in Asia, where it has been known to hunt humans deliberately.

Brazilian Wandering Spider
The world's deadliest, most fearsome spider, this big, hairy South American creepy crawly has a killer bite.

Komodo Dragon
The world's biggest lizard can catch and eat large prey. It is found only on small islands in Indonesia.

Blue-Ringed Octopus
One of the world's smallest but most venomous octopuses, it lives in reefs and rock pools around Asia and Australia.

Brown Bear
Found across northern parts of the world, brown bears are big, savage, strong, and incredibly fearsome.

Saltwater Crocodile
The world's biggest and deadliest crocodile, this green giant prowls the oceans—and rivers and swamps.

Black Mamba
This beast gets top spot for its speed, aggression, but most of all its deadly venom. A black mamba bite can kill a person in 20 minutes, and is always fatal if left untreated.

GLOSSARY

Acid - A chemical that can dissolve other substances.

Aggressive - Easily made angry and likely to attack.

Allergy - A dangerous reaction in the body to a particular substance.

Bacteria - Tiny living things that can sometimes cause diseases.

Bone marrow - Soft, fatty substance found inside some bones.

Camouflage - Markings or colors that help an animal blend in with its surroundings.

Cannibalism - The eating of other animals of the same species.

Captivity - Being kept in a zoo, aquarium, or other enclosed space.

Carrion - Flesh of dead animals.

Cephalopod - Family of animals that includes octopuses and squid.

Colubrid - Family of snakes that includes boomslangs and twig snakes.

Constrictor - Group of snakes that squeeze their prey to death.

Coral reef - Shell-like structure built in the sea by tiny sea creatures called coral polyps.

Echinoderm - Group of sea creatures that includes starfish and sea urchins.

Elapid - Family of snakes that includes kraits and mambas.

Funeral pyre - A fire for burning a dead body, sometimes built on a riverbank.

Immune - Unable to be harmed by something.

Indigenous - Native to a particular area or land.

Intestines - Tubes that carry food along inside the body, also called guts.

Larva - The baby stage of some types of insects.

Mustelid - Family of mammals that includes weasels and otters.

Nematocysts - Stinging cells found on the tentacles of jellyfish.

Parasite - A creature that lives on or takes its food from another living thing.

Pits - Holes on the heads of some snakes, used for sensing the body heat of prey.

Pollinate - To spread pollen from one plant to another, which helps plants make seeds.

Predator - An animal that hunts and eats other animals.

Prey - An animal that is hunted and eaten by another animal.

Proboscis - Long, tubelike mouth.

Raptor - Another name for a bird of prey.

Scavenge - To search for leftovers, garbage, or dead animals as food.

Streamlined - Having a long, smooth, rounded shape to move easily through water or air.

Talons - Sharp claws, especially those of birds.

Tenacious - Stubborn and good at not letting go.

Tentacles - Long, trailing, or dangling body parts found on animals such as jellyfish and squid.

Toxin - A poison.

INDEX